Café Millennium
& Other Poems

Café Millennium
& Other Poems

H.R. Stoneback

Cover Art Design by Dona Simons

Grateful acknowledgements are due to the editors of the
following publications where some of these poems first
appeared: *Aethlon, Arete, Cape Rock, Fan, The North
Dakota Quarterly, The Shawangunk Review, The Tinker,
The W.B. Yeats Society Newsletter.* "Cartographers of the
Deus Loci" appeared in limited edition hardcover from
Bird & Bull Press (Philadelphia 1982). "Woodsmoke in
Aigues-Mortes" appeared in a trilingual broadside (translated
into French and Provencal) from Edicioun Lou Gregau (13460
France). "Petanque Poems" appeared as a chapbook (bilingual
facing-page translation English/Provencal) from Edicioun Lou
Gregau (1997). "Toad Suck Ferry" appeared in the anthology
Traveling America with Today's Poets (MacMillan, 1976).

Published by Portals Press
4411 Fontainebleau Drive
New Orleans, Louisiana 70125
USA

Library of Congress Catalogue Card Number
00-135731

ISBN 0-916620-84-0

This book is for my father
David M. Stoneback
(1909-1970)
Musician, Poet, Factory Worker

Table of Contents

Café Millennium

In a café in Paris, we are discussing
The Millennium, the dead century.
They seem cheerful about the next century,
Agree that it has to be better, cannot
Be worse than this, the bloodiest in history.
Then she says: "I don't know. This century was Ordinary
In its Evil. Stalin, Hitler, Mao -- all mass
Murderers were just Ordinary, just Nature
Doing its thing. Why must we make them extraordinary?
That can only be true if you cling to a notion
Of God, who you hold accountable for all
Suffering Nature. All this poetry that says NO
To Suffering, to Nature, is so tiresome."
She sips her wine. She is a philosopher,
An atheist, and a novelist, in that order.
Then he says: "But Oh the Horror! This has been
The most horrific century ever
and we must raise our voices,
Say NO, in poetry, song and prayer: all poetry is prayer --
What's the use of not believing, not singing?
It's the only thing that makes us Human."
He sips his wine. He is a poet, a philosopher,
And an intermittent believer, in that order.
I sip my wine. I say nothing.

Then the youngest among us says: "The only
Available and availing prayer now is poetry.
God isn't listening. He went away in 1941
When he smelled the satanic incense from Auschwitz.
He stayed away when he caught the odious whiff
Of thirty million dead in Brave New China
And the Killing Fields of Cambodia.
And he isn't coming back.
What's the use of believing in anything but poetry?
If you believe in God you cannot write
The poetry we need now." She sips her wine.
She is Director of an MFA Program

At an American university,
A teacher, and a poet, in that order.
I sip my wine, thinking about the routine
Dailiness of Evil,
The terror of Nature, the savage century,
The Scandal of Suffering, the possibilities of prayer
And poetry, and the horror of some MFA Programs.
I sip my wine and say nothing. I am a singer,
A teacher, a believer in wine (and some other things),
And a poet-songwriter,
In no particular order.
And I am thinking of a song.

I am thinking of a song I might write
On my way home, walking by (maybe through) Notre Dame,
Walking home in the small sweet rain, Home
Where the House Wine is better than the Café Millennium.
Yet still, it's not time to leave, because somehow
I love this café, I love these people
I am talking with, saying nothing with. . .
I love this Dailiness of Being Human,
Love the people I am saying NO to Nothing with. . .

Café Y2K: The Menu

"The problem," she says, handing me the menu,
"Is all these people saying Yes to Nothing —
Almost everybody, locked in orgasmic
Embrace with Nada, orgiastic caress of nothingness."
I smile, nod, study the clever menu:
Apocalypticism du Jour
Solipsism a la Carte
Cons (u) mmations Diverse
Les Milkshakes Americain
Grace Under Pression.
"It looks as if the Patron is a failed
Student of Literary Theory," I say.
"It is to be hoped," she says, eyeing
The menu, "that he's not a Ph.D.,
That Nietzsche is not Chef in his kitchen,
That Derrida is not head bartender."
I read aloud: "Pizza Feu de Bois Millénaire.
Quik-Snacks: Croque Monsieur (le sandwich
Bill Clinton), Croque Madame (le sandwich
Hillary), Croque Interne (le sandwich Monica) —"
"I wish they would," she interrupts. "Just croak,
Just go away." "It isn't funny any more."
"It never was." We fold the soiled menus.

"What will you do New Year's Eve," she asks.
"I'll be singing, or reading poetry
At The End of the World Bar in Bimini."
She shuts her eyes. "No, it's not Y2K-Chic,
It's always been called that. It's just a shack
On the beach, sand floor. On islands, at least,
They have a good chance of knowing it's always,
Every day, every moment, the End,
Or the Beginning of the World. . ." "I like
The Way You Speak In Capital Letters."
She smiles, touches her glass to mine gently.
"What will you do New Year's Eve?" I ask.
"I might read a book, might sleep on the beach,
Might sail to some island in the sun."

"'Where my people have toiled since time begun'" --
I sing "And what shall we do next year?" "What shall
We ever do?" "I'll just keep on gardening,
Writing, singing." "I might make a pilgrimage,
St.-Jacques, audience with the Pope, Assisi."
"You're not Catholic?" "Not yet. Not really.
But I've always wanted to go to Assisi.
I want to pray there, not in my head, on my knees."
"Assisi, Bimini — right now let's cross the street —

They have good wine there. I know the sommelier.
Wine's as good as any place to start to pray."

The Sommelier Speaks

"This is a fine St.-Chinian Reserve
I think you'll like. Deep goût de terroir.
I know the man who makes it. A faithful friend."
The Sommelier is a man who can use words
Like faithful and make them sound new. He smiles
As we taste the peppery, velvety wine.
"Oh it's a lovely wine," she says prayerfully.
"Thank you and thank God," he says, in his way
Of saying ancient things that he makes new.
He goes away. Comes back with Provençal olives,
Dry-roasted with garlic, and saucisson.

"1999 should be a fine vintage in the Midi.
I will lay down many wines that we will drink
In 2009, maybe even 2029."
We mention the wine, the menu across the street.
He shudders: "That place. It has been there five
Minutes and will soon disappear. Here, we will
Keep doing as we have for centuries.
You know our name, our menu, has not changed
Since before the Revolution. They" — he shoots
A sneer across the street — "They know nothing."
"That's what we were just talking about," she says.

"The thing is this," he says: "All Apocalypticism
Is Mere Solipsism. Time is not tired.
They all confuse personal weariness
With the earth, take the Radical Human
Insufficiency and transpose it to the Cosmos.
The confusion of the merely personal
With sociocultural necessity,
With historical inevitability,
Has caused many problems, worked much Evil.
Consider Marx, Lenin, Hitler, Stalin, Mao.
They knew nothing about wine, about time."

He went away and I wrote down what he said
On a wine-stained napkin. "Would it be merely

Personal," she asked, "if I said I loved
This wine. Him. You. The World?" "No, that would be prayer."
The Sommelier returned, with a silver tray,
Acolyte, priest, bearing a sacrament.
"Here is something to erase your unpleasant
Experience across the street." He poured the wine,
Placed some chevre on some rough darkgold peasant bread.
We swirled in silence, tasted the goat-cheese.
We held our glasses to the candlelight,

Breathed the earth and sun and then we tasted:
Massive, deep purple, profound berry-coffee-
Licorice-spicy-richness. "It is Pomerol '82.
Rather fine, yes? We'll drink it again in 2009.
If we start with such wine the rest will slowly,
Slowly happen." He went away, came back
In streetclothes, handed me a bottle.
I looked at the label: Trotanoy '82.
"A gift for you to celebrate the New Old World.
I must go say a prayer for my suffering brother.
Drink this New Year's Eve and pray for me, for all of us."

At the Café Millennium with Aldington, Durrell, Faulkner, Fitzgerald, Hemingway and Pound *

> (A multimedia performance work: poetry, prose, song, in different voices)**
>
> Someone said: "The dead writers are remote from us because we know so much more than they did." Precisely, and they are that which we know.
>
> T.S. Eliot "Tradition and the Individual Talent"
>
> I still miss someone. . .
> Johnny Cash

The Garden is in good order
in spite of the terrible storm,
the terror of the night before.
I sit at the Café Millennium alone,
reading: "Literature is the only authentic
Time Machine. Story, song, poetry,
and those who make it bend and transcend time."
The critic's words, heavier than song,
tell me what I've known all along
so I close the journal, hear the jukebox:
Piaf is singing "Non! Je ne regrette rien. . ."
  And I am not at all surprised when she walks through the Café,
or when Fitzgerald, Hemingway and Pound, followed by Faulkner,
Aldington and Durrell, enter the umbrella-dappled shade. "Everything
authentic is simultaneous," I scribble on my beer coaster, and put it in
my pocket as they join me at my table. The waiter, poised like the
keeper of the mysteries, takes orders: pastis, wine, whiskey, olives,
bread, saucisson. Hemingway softly sings, a little offkey. "Rien de
rien" — Durrell harmonizes in his ethereal Irish-Buddhist lilting chant.
Then Hemingway says: "Rien de rien. It's the only Way to Everything."
Pound reads a letter from Yeats, something about visions and Phase 22

---

* Many of the events and conservations transcribed in this work really happened; others are invented. The reader may feel free to decide what is invented, what happened. Provide your own footnotes.
** This performance work premièred at the International Richard Aldington Conference in les Saintes-Maries-de-la-Mer, France (June 23, 2000). The formal World Première was at the International Lawrence Durrell Conference in Corfu, Greece (July 4, 2000).

of the Millennium. Fitzgerald says "He's crazy!" Scott looks worried,
is rude to the waiter when he brings drinks. Faulkner lights his pipe,
says nothing. Aldington proclaims: "I have left England forever."

see, they return, one, and by one
see, they return, and bring us with them
they have not returned they have never left us

Ezra pulls out a manuscript, writes all over the pages.
Hemingway looks over his shoulder, watches like a cat.
I lean over, see Ezra circle "perhaps" in the manuscript
and scrawl in the margin "Perhaps be damned."
On another page he underlines "perhaps"
scribbles "dam per'apsez" and "make up yr. mind. . .
if you know *know* damn well or else you don't."
He looks up from the manuscript, proclaims
"Perhaps is an ugly word" (Hemingway says:
"It's worse on the end of your cigar").
Ezra rants about perhaps, all writers must avoid
it — "Damn Per Apses!" He pounds the table.
Fitzgerald says "Sometimes you have to approach
the high altar through the apse." Durrell says:
"That could be construed as a form of buggery."
Pound holds up the manuscript, shows the title page around the table,
points to the top where it says "HE DO THE POLICE IN DIFFERENT
VOICES: Part I. THE BURIAL OF THE DEAD." This whole first
page is crossed out. Pound shows another title page. This one has
another title and an epigraph passage that ends "The horror! the horror!"
Ezra says: "I told him to lose the Conrad, not weighty enough to stand
the citation." He passes the manuscript around, saying "It's damn
good, about enough to make the rest of us shut up shop." Faulkner
passes the manuscript on to Aldington without looking, puffs his pipe
in silence, looks off toward the fountain, where kids sail toy boats on
the pond.

Durrell and Aldington are singing:
"C'est payé, Balayé, Oublié. . ."
Aldington slides the manuscript to Durrell without looking
at it. Durrell stops singing, says: "The salt of a poem
holds on, even in empty weather." He puts his hand flat

on top of the manuscript, reads and rubs the page, says:
"Tread softly, for here you stand on miracle ground."

The waiter scrupulously orchestrates
the empty tables and chairs.
Piaf is singing again: "Je repars à zéro. . ."
I get up singing, walk over to the loo
to make some notes before I forget what Ez said.
I'm standing by the phone scribbling when Faulkner
walks by, stops, asks: "You writing a poem?"
"No, just phone numbers, sir. I called the Muse
But couldn't get through. Last time I talked to her
she says 'Sorry it's that time of the month Bubba.'
She tells me to try Gingko Biloba."
"All the phone lines are down," Faulkner says,
"that terrific storm. And besides the Muse
does not accept collect calls. You have to pay
with mysterious Hermetic Tokens."
He walks on by, humming "Swing Low, Sweet Chariot."
I write: "Before I finish this sentence
the Century will turn, the Millennium will burn."
I cross the last part out, write "see, they return
remember that I have remembered"

Echoing through the Garden from our table
I hear the voice of Uncle Ez droning:
"All ideas are suspicious of the facts.
All particulars confound the abstract."
Hemingway says: "Yes. Absolutely."
I sit down between Ernest and Ezra.
Pound's old once-black coat has the friction-glazed
greenish cast of old house flies.
Cigarette and pipe smoke coils like barbed wire,
under the umbrellas of yesterday
over the tables of tomorrow.
A gang of goosestepping pigeons scratch vague
swastikas in the sand near the table.
Ezra shuffles his feet, chasing them,
erasing their calligraphy:
"That is not what I meant, not what I meant at all,"

he mumbles to no one in particular.
Then he starts humming, in low steady
trembly monotone. This means, we all know,
he is composing.
He has always done this. Yeats has always done this.
The two of them living in that cold Stone Cottage
on the forlorn heath, humming, composing.

> *oh what is that noise in the chimney*
> *is it only the wind the answer my friend*
> *Yeats and Pound are composing again*

Ezra gets up to go to the W.C., humming past the other tables,
where eyes lift, slide, watch him pass. Hemingway says: "He's crazy
but he wasn't always. He's crazy now but he was kind and generous
and I love him still." Aldington agrees emphatically: "He was very
good to me." Then Durrell chants:

"The ancient songs pass deathward mournfully. . ."
Richard says: "When I wrote that poem
I was 19 and Ezra called me The Faun."
"Did you hate to be called The Faun?" Durrell asks.
"It was OK, at 19, when H.D. was around
with Ezra calling her Dryad." Larry sings again:
"'The ancient songs pass deathward mournfully' --
I was reading where troops stood up in the trenches
during the Great War and roared that poem, is that true?"
"I'm afraid it is. My greatest hit.
A terrible fate to be remembered for a century
for something you wrote when you were 19."
Aldington drains his wineglass, lifts it to the light:
"I would prefer to build the crystal world."
I feel in my pocket his daughter's edition of Aldington's *A Dream
in the Luxembourg* signed with love from Catha. I came here to
the Garden today to read it here and now all these characters have
delayed the project in my pocket but I feel it there, half-remembering
lines I skimmed on the Metro: "daydreaming under the trees in the
Luxembourg." And what did he say about being the "slow northern
type," how, being English, his espirit didn't even get on the escalier;
and asking "Was it only a dream in the Luxembourg?" And how

he knelt to the ground after clouds from the North swallowed the sun
and put a pinch of dust to his lips — "It had a very bitter taste." I take
a pinch of dust from the Luxembourg ground, touch it to my lips.
Aldington smiles at me. I will have to read it again and write to Catha.
I feel Aldington's dream in my pocket, near my heart, and I love this
exiled Man of Letters, this poet-soldier of the Holy Earth, even if
everybody calls him Top Grumpy and thinks him bitter. There must be
something very fine about a man who is censored by England, ostra-
cized by British twits in that tight little isle.

> *before I finish this poem, the millennium will turn*
> *remember that I have remembered*
> *everything authentic is simultaneous*

My mind wanders from the talk at the table
I hear far voices saying
"I wanted an audience with the Pope
I made the Pilgrimage to Rome
But the Old Boy wasn't home"
"I went to Assisi"
"I should have gone to the Abruzzi"
I hear my voice say "I went to Brindisi
where Virgil died suddenly
on his way home from Greece
next to the Hertz Rental Car Office"
saying it coldchill-spooked and thinking
the rains of remorse resonate on tin roofs
of memory like pebbles scattered, stones
of the past sautéed in the skillet of my skull
then *yeah right scribble that line and let Ezra edit it*
Ezra is back, still humming. Everyone is quiet.
We sit in the unchanging light
the light of 2000 (or 1900 or 1800)
the unchanging light of every fin de siècle
the dappled speckled heckling
light and suddenly I know it is 1899
we are *une tranche de vie*
we are, with the bread and olives and wine,
a *nature mort*
and behind us the can-can skirts, Baudelaire,

purple lobsters on leashes, laughter, accordions
foretelling the unthinkable Somme
the sickening sums of Verdun
what's coming what's coming now
China North Korea Iraq Africa falling towers
California New York London Moscow leaning spires
  And Richard says: "Ten million dead, twenty million crippled
  in four years. What song from the trenches now?" And I see
  he is talking to me so we must be in the year 2000. And I list
  the statistics: "Let's see — since World War Two, you caught
  the 30 million murdered in China by Great Leaps, right? And
  one-third of the total population of Cambodia exterminated
  by ideology? And all the others murdered by their own sons and
  daughters, brothers and sisters in mad abstract revolutionary rage?"
  "Yes," Hemingway says. "We know that." "What about right now?"
  Faulkner asks. "At this exact moment? — Genocide and so-called
  Civil War everywhere. Guerillas, so-called Freedom Fighters hack
  the limbs from women and children. Murderous tribal abandon.
  Today, 22 million refugees and 30 million internally displaced persons.
  Tomorrow more. In California, rebirth therapists, proclaiming New
  Age adjustment, suffocate children in simulated wombs. Kids glutted
  with video games. Schools on fire. What else do you want to know?
  Adults confuse e-mail with letters, the Internet with knowledge.
  Language is dying — almost nobody reads, nobody writes. Is that what
  you want to hear?" "Then it will be even worse," Larry says, "when
  this generation and the next pull the levers and the triggers." And then
  it is the Year 2099 or 2100 and we all avert our gaze in silence.

Behind the conversation I watch the fountains,
the pond like a noonbright sea, the spray
like promiscuous surf in the tree-dazed August Garden
the afternoon is a sleepy cat stretching
yawning with the fierceness of futurity.
I meditate the genealogy of the trees
feeling oaks and sycamores, marronniers and locusts,
reconstructing their ancient urban past
inscribing the Scarecrow of the Arbored Mind
filling in the branches of their Family Human

Ezra is talking about fencing with Yeats

about reading aloud to him at Stone Cottage
all of Wordsworth whom they loathed
only less than Milton and Whitman
"Wordsworth was a silly old sheep,"
Ezra says, "but he did have a certain genius
for *imagisme*
for particularity, strong clean images
but buried in a desert of sheep-bleatings."
   They discuss all this, and imagism, as a group of tourists passes by
led by a guide barking his spiel like some nitwit creepy commander
from some dim Uganda of the soul. No one recognizes the famous
visages at our table. Two Brits sit down at the next table, talking loud,
excited, gesturing. They talk about the darling flowers in the Garden,
the darling dogs walking by, darling this, darling that. The Darling
Garden. The taller one says "History is darling once it's over."
His companion says "The 20s were darling." And his companion says
"I rather think the 50s were more darling, and oh those darling 60s."
We sit in silence at our table. We all look at each other and at the next
table. After they leave Aldington says "Darling Brit Twits." Ezra says:
"The kind that are bad for a writer's career. Perhaps we should ban
the word darling along with per apse." Richard says: "It's no worse,
properly used, than 'delicate.' Remember when you used 'delicate' 947
times in *Lustra*?" "That was before I stretched my voodoocabulary.
I have you to thank for that. We all have our favorite words."
Faulkner studies the myriad effluvia of the fountain.
Fitzgerald dreams in orgiastic gorgeousness,
though Romish shadows of hieratic guilt cross
his brow. Durrell summons the miracle
of the Deus Loci from his glass.
Hemingway says nothing, clean and true and silent.

Then she walks towards us walking through the Garden
like a chapter in a Russian novel
she brings a blizzard of cool into the café
Larry says "I want some ice cream
though I detest it" — he has been watching her
since she emerged from the Station of the Metro
in the distance by the Garden gates
the subject is changed
the vanilla ecstasy of the blonde assassin

the café's deliquescence
history melts away and Aldington is The Faun again
Pound looks like Pan
Durrell is Pater's Satyr
Larry says: "presence long since divined. . .and waited for —
Oh Miracle Ground — the heart must be very old
to feel so young." Fitzgerald looks worried.
Faulkner smokes his pipe, fondles his pipe attentively.
Hemingway gets up, follows her into the green pavilion
of the café —- she talks to the waiter, then turns
and leaves, goes back to the Metro
taking the underground with her —
Ezra sighs, then starts humming again
Durrell adjusts his shorts
reprivatizing his privates
Richard eyes him: "Try underwear, Larry."
"Writers don't wear underwear," Hemingway says.
Faulkner stares at Papa.

   Scott is very worried, starts talking fast about Zelda. She's been
visiting friends in the country a few days; he hasn't been able to reach
her. All the phones are down after the storm. He takes out his laptop,
goes to the next table, tries to e-mail Zelda, tries her on his cell-phone.
No luck. He comes back to our table, tosses off his drink. His face
tightens, his eyes sink, his skin looks like used candle wax. He is
passing out, or dying, sitting up. Hemingway stands, takes Scott
under one arm, motions for me to get the other. We walk Scott towards
the Garden gate.

"*Doucement,*" Ernest says. "*Doucement* but hold him tight."
(Oh softly now. Softly for us all)
"We'll get him in a taxi. He'll be all right."
Ernest dips his hand in the last fountain,
the small one by the gate path, gently dabs
cool water on Scott's forehead (those of us who know
walk very slowly and walk with each other
in infinite love and compassion)
We get Scott in a taxi. He seems OK.
   I say: "He's been very quiet." Ernest says: "He's been worried about
Zelda." Papa says he is holding Barrera seats for me at the next Fiesta.
"And I'm expecting you for the marlin off Havana. And how's your
writing going?" We walk back to the Café, see four women standing

by our table. It's Zelda and Sparrow and Mary Hemingway and
somebody I don't know. Ernest says she's some French Countess.
Their backs are turned to us. From behind, with her hair cut very short,
Mary looks like a boy until she turns around in that sweater. Sparrow
felt me coming, and turned first. We all greet each other with
Trinitarian kisses. Only Zelda does not kiss Hemingway. Zelda flirts
with everybody but Hemingway. Durrell flirts with Sparrow. Mary
flirts with me. Zelda seems happy that Scott is not there. She walks off
with Faulkner, like some insidious Eula Varner.

The fountain's accent shifts
the way the sea's spindrift language,
merging with particular islands, changes.
The waiter rearranges tables and chairs,
singing, composing the late afternoon.
Clouds form, promising the weather of poems.
A light wind rises, ripples the trees
like an incipient narrative epiphany.
The women are talking about the terrible storm the night before.
The Countess says: "I took the lightning personally." Zelda says:
"I loved it." Mary says: "The thunder-rumble erased all history,
the lightning-blitz made me tremble with terror." Sparrow says:
"All terror is local." Hemingway says he was with James Joyce —
"And Joyce was scared, he always is in thunderstorms, reminds me
of a defrocked priest out in a storm taking the lightning personally."
Aldington says "All the lines went dead, cables crashed to the ground.
Telephone poles and hesistant hellos terrified by the silence, the farewell
wave of ancient trees in some vast amnesiac valley." "Shell-shocked,
hell-shocked," Ezra says. "Smell-shocked," Durrell says, "the smell
of the lightning striking the rose arch, the orange fireball scalding
two hundred blooming roses in a split second." "And now we sit here,"
the Countess says, "in the Garden of Amnesia." "The Garden of Aphasia,"
Larry says. "Never confuse aphasia with aphagia," Ezra instructs;
"Eupepsia is the Poet's Passport." "Eupepsia-Cola," I say. Zelda drags
Faulkner away again; she is walking barefoot now like some sinister
Lena Grove, Faulkner holding her sandals. When I go to the W.C. to see
what they're doing behind the trees, Faulkner follows me. Standing at the
urinal, Faulkner says: "You know she's plumb crazy." "Yes," I say,
"Ernest told me." Then he says: "I liked your essay on *Go Down, Moses*.
You nailed it, dead on. When you gonna write about *The Sound and the Fury*?"

"Thank you kindly," I say, "I've been savin' that." And I look at Faulkner thinking how can I tell him how it felt thirty-some years ago when I was a surf-crazed singer trashy-troubadour-college-dropout-poet in Hawaii and I housesat for the guy who had all of Faulkner's books even the rare stuff and I read everything he ever wrote in about three weeks and I knew that everything was changed nothing would ever be the same again like riding the biggest wave you ever dreamed of making it impossible to write fiction for a long time maybe never you bastard you but I'm a better poet-singer than you and that's what you say you always wanted to be and failed but YES SIR you changed everything and all I can say out loud is "Thank you kindly, Sir" as we walk back to the table. Silence with Faulkner (and Hemingway) is always comfortable.

Larry is still flirting with Sparrow
asking her to sing, shifting in his shorts

The Countess stands up, excuses herself, says "I have a train to catch," walks away, turns, calls Sparrow and me over. She says to Sparrow: "Never trust a writer, especially one who can't sing. Don't trust Larry. He'll use you. He uses people." "Doesn't almost everybody?" Sparrow says. "I love him anyway." "They call him a leading Writer-on-Love-in-the-Modern-World," the Countess says, "but he doesn't know how to love, only how to use." She slings her large clear plastic bag of croissants over her shoulder. "I'm off to my country-place," she says. "Do come down and visit soon. Don't worry about what I said. We all have our croissants to bear. Stay unfuckable, especially around writers. Except this one. Write me a poisson-pen letter and tell me all the gossip." She kisses us both three times and walks away fast, the Garden leaning after her. "So," I say, "Larry was hitting on you?" "Yes," Sparrow says, "and what were you and Faulkner doing in the John?" "Very funny. You sound like Zelda." "If you must know," Sparrow says, "we were talking about Sappho. About what he told me that time at his house right after he lost her. And then I told him how, not long after visiting his grave, we came home and lost our daughter. His eyes got big and wet and he said nobody knows do they and then he said would I be his daughter and he hugged me and called me Daughter. That's when you came back and the Countess got up and left. You call that hitting on me?" "OK," I say, "but watch out if Hemingway starts calling you Daughter" and I laugh but I am thinking as we go back to the table

oh all the lost and longed-for daughters
see they return they have not returned
they never left us remember that I have remembered
everything authentic is simultaneous and all
terror is local like a tree like a telephone pole

"Sing a song, Sparrow," Larry says. "Sing those songs
you sang in my kitchen at Sommières, Daughter."
Looking at me, she says "we need a guitar."
 Aldington says the waiter has a guitar behind the bar. Richard gets up,
 goes inside the café, comes back with a small guitar, hands it to me.
 I tune it. Larry says: "Sing 'Barbara Allen', Daughter." I hit the opening
 E-chord arpeggio, then softly hammer-ride the E-minor into the E
 three times and Sparrow starts to sing:
  "In Scarlet Town where I was born
  There was a fair maid dwellen
  Made every youth cry well-away
  And her name was Barbara Allen. . .
  Hard-hearted Barbara Allen. . .
  And on her grave a bri-i-ar."
Trees lean and listen
in the fountain's suspension
the waiter motionless
poised with timestopped tray in midair
 as Sparrow sings only the six crucial stanzas of the long hard old story and
 Richard moves his lips singing softly Ernest and Faulkner move their lips
 soundlessly and Pound hums and Mary and Zelda sing soft harmony on
 the words Barbara Allen and Larry just watches Sparrow. The song over,
 in the silence Larry says: "There's something Fifth-Dimensional, a mystical
 tremor in your voice. . ." Ezra finally says "Old Willie Shakespeare used to
 sing that song." Hemingway says "Here he comes" — we all watch as
 Shakespeare walks by, one arm on Kit Marlowe's shoulders, the other on
 Ben Jonson's. They are singing "Barbara Allen." They do not see us, walk
 on by, singing. "Hardhearted," Richard says, pronouncing the slow bonezero
 chillword as in a mystical chant, "Hardheartedness." "Women, shee-ut,"
 Faulkner drawls Missippily redneck-laughingly then says softer: "My
 grandmother used to sing that song." "Mine, too," Sparrow says. Mary
 says: "But you forgot the rose *around* the briar verse." "We didn't forget,"
 Sparrow says, "it doesn't exist where we come from." "In the Kentucky
 Mountains," I say, "we don't have no truck with entwining roses and briars
 in sentimental-slithery graveyards." "All Souths are the same," Ezra says.

"All hard songs endure in the sun's southernness." Larry says: "The heart must be very old to be so young." Ernest says: "Nothing is ever lost." Larry says: "Nothing is ever lost."

I say: "Red Warren always said that too." Hemingway says: "I took Red Warren and Allen Tate to the bicycle races and Mass at St.-Sulpice. No, Tate went to Mass with me, but Warren wouldn't go. Tate also said 'Nothing is ever lost'. He still owes me 30 francs from the bicycle races." I say: "Everything authentic is simultaneous. Even unpaid debts."

Larry wants to sing: "Sing another kitchen song, Daughter. That one about flying away."
I hit the opening licks and Sparrow sings:
> "Some glad morning when this life is over
> I'll fly away. . .
> Like a bird from prison bars has flown. . .
> I'll fly away Oh Glory I'll fly away
> When I die Hallelujah by-and-by
> I'll fly away"

After the first chorus everybody sings along. Zelda sings it right from the start, stealing my harmony lines. She knows all the words--it's an Alabama kind of song. I have a vision of her, all dressed in black, home from the asylum, standing on the street corner in Montgomery, handing out religious tracts, singing "I'll Fly Away." I wonder if she gave a tract to that kid singing in her deltadawn streets, if he sang "I'll Fly Away" with her, that skinny kid Hank Williams. Ezra says: "I always wanted to fly. Dreamed of it for a long time." "Me too," Richard says. "I did fly," Larry says. "I dreamed of falling for years," I say, "but since the age of 30 I've always dreamed of flying."

The fat Fascist pigeons are back, goosestepping
around the table. A gigantic orange cat lurks
beneath the next table, frozen, intent,
a trembletailed tiger stalking a traitor
at the ultimate Last Supper
Mary leans toward me, runs her fingers across the strings of the guitar.
I offer it to her. She takes it, plays a few chords. She has to watch her
fingers form the chords. Hemingway watches her like a cat--I know that
look--he's afraid she's getting drunk. Mary says: "Show me what you just
did on the bottom strings in that last song. Put my fingers in the right place."
I reach around behind her, put her left hand fingers in the right places, show
her what to do with her right hand. She smells like some kind of tropical

vine. Or maybe it's just all that hair coloring she uses. She keeps trying
to get it right, her fingers following mine. I remember what Bill Walton told
me about Mary. I know this position well. Used to give guitar lessons 10 to
20 bucks an hour. Advertised on the radio in Alabama--played a fancy lick,
said in tall Radio Voice "If you want to pick guitar like this--dom dum dum
doom--call Stoney at this number." Ernest watches our hands on the neck
of the guitar.

The pigeons are cooing and kazooing
and the cat pounces, missing: jumping high, twisting,
after the clumsy pigeon's thrumming heavy-winged takeoff.
Hemingway charms the cat, picks it up,
holds it against his chest in that same
position he used to hold "Crazy Christian"
his favorite cat of fifty-five.

Durrell says: "Sparrow, please sing that song, Daughter,
that one about the circle that can't be broken."
I hit the opening licks on the guitar
and Sparrow sends the song soaring into the sky:
    "Will the Circle be Unbroken
    By-and-by Lord by-and-by. . .
    In the sky, Lo-ord, in the sky. . .
    I said to the undertaker. . .
    Lord I hate to see her go. . .
    Will the Circle be Unbroken. . ."
Zelda sings along, tries some crazy throaty alto gospel harmony, biting some
of my usual notes. After Sparrow gets the song in gear, everybody sings and
hums the chorus. Ezra hums all the way through. Ernest and his cat purr.
Mary moves her lips, watches my fingers on the guitar. Parisian passersby
form a circle around our table, smiling, clapping hands, singing along;
our waiter sings, too, doing an elegant turn and strut past our table, the tray
fingertip-raised above his head. I think of New Orleans and street jazz
funerals. The waiter turns. We all love this waiter. When the song fades,
the crowd applauds. Nobody is famous here, we are all in the circle together.
Deep shade swallows the café, it is getting late. Sparrow shivers in her light
sleeveless silk blouse. Durrell puts his arm around her. She says: "That looks
like a nice warm shirt, Larry." He takes it off--you know the shirt, the one
he wears in all the documentary films, all the pictures there toward the end--
they stand up, he's shorter than Sparrow, but the shirt fits, he helps her put
it on, they hug each other tight.

Writers, the best ones, always give us the shirts
off their backs; sometimes we accept the gift,
not sure how to wear it, how to make it fit.

* * *

After the alphabet of apéritifs
The syntax of suffering and song
The grammar of greatness and grace under *pression*
The amen of almonds and olives and *saucisson*
The Nunc Dimittis of Pastis
It is time to leave the Garden.
We talk about tomorrow, when we'll all be back at the Café Millennium.
They will all be on the Imus in the Morning Show, a special program on
Writers-of-the-Century. They wonder about it. I tell them nothing about
the I-Man except he's damn good at making books best-sellers. They all
have their doubts about television and radio talk shows, all except Larry
who espouses the virtues of TV for book-sales. I try to envision Aldington,
Durrell, Faulkner, Fitzgerald, Hemingway and Pound on TV--maybe
Jeopardy or PassWord or What's My Line would be better or Wheel of
Fortune with all the phrases taken from their books, with Vanna doing her
iambic minidress heel-clicking pentameter letter-walk, delphic oracle
revealing their lines: "Miracle Ground" and "Deus Loci"; "Death, we turn
to thee, singing One last song" and "the undying sea and the Holy Earth!";
"There died a myriad. . .for an old bitch. . .for a botched civilization";
"She smelled like trees"; "Her voice was full of money"; "Face to face for
the last time in history with something commensurate to man's capacity
for wonder" (let's see Vanna turn over all those letters); "Not merely endure,
he will prevail"; "Isn't it pretty to think so?" "Nick said nothing. . .he was
in his home where he had made it." All I tell them about tomorrow is that
Imus sells books. We finish our drinks. Sparrow hugs Larry's shirt tight
around her while Ezra drones "The Song of the Shirt."

We leave, our waiter bows, we stroll through the Garden,
down the avenues of tall dark trees
past the sculpted queen with the flowing gown,
her head cocked and chin lifted like a cat's
when you scratch its chin, the large cross
resting between her perfect stone breasts
(and you still love her as you love Houdon's *La Frileuse*)

and Sparrow holds the shirt tight around her breasts.
We pause by the boules-ground where Socratic boulistes
say benedictions over the game that goes on forever.
We say farewell to Faulkner, to Mary and Zelda and Ernest--
they go through the gates on the St.-Sulpice side
down toward where they live and they are singing,
their arms around each other, even Ernest and Zelda at last.
We circle the Garden to leave on the Boul Mich side
through the great gold-tipped iron gates
where the guards stand ready to close the Garden
a sight that Ezra says terrifies him:
"Terror is local
Error is universal
And--chez moi-- very local also.
Is there, in the austere eye of history, any way
to atone for, to expiate?"
Larry stops singing, says:
"Music is Love in search of a word."
"You stole that from Sidney Lanier," I say.
He laughs: "Tell the whole world of my theft!"
"I already have." We laugh, repeat the phrase
together—"Music is Love in search of a word."
Larry sees MacNiven, his biographer,
on the far side of the street and waves as if
the boulevard were time and he at the end of the street.
Ezra chants: "The poem is song in the terror of time,
fleeing mere words, seeking the condition of no less
than infinite limitless love to redeem the line
all in the unbroken unspoken circle."

We embrace farewells until tomorrow
and Sparrow starts to take off, return the garment,
but Larry says "Keep it. You wear it well."
She says: "Music is Love in search of a shirt."
They go down, Richard, Larry, and Ezra,
into the Station of the Metro.
We stroll home happy to our place on the rue Saint-Jacques.
The Café Millennium is closed, but we'll return, we'll all be back

II

"The Next Day at the Café with Dylan, Fats, Imus, Jerry Jeff, Hank: Writers, Singers & the Imus Show"

Now maybe Stoney was a liar, yeah, no doubt about it
But just the way he told things made you never want to doubt him
'Cause he kept you going when the road got rough
And he brought you through all the lean times by making it up
— Jerry Jeff Walker "Stoney" (from the road,
an oft-recorded road-song of the 1960s)

Every song you truly sing, every story truly told, costs you
one day of your life. But you got to keep singing, telling,
making it up like life, like everything, depended on the song,
the story. It's precision and passion, it ain't lying, except
in that way they mean when they say "Art's the Lie that tells
the Truth." And it can't be self-serving, has to somehow serve
others. That's the only truth I know so far.
— Stoney (from a Bourbon Street Club, onstage
betweensong talk, New Orleans 1963)

What thou lovest well remains,
the rest is dross. . .
Pull down thy vanity, it is not man
Made courage, or made order, or made grace,
Pull down thy vanity, I say pull down.
Learn of the green world what can be thy place
In scaled invention or true artistry.
— Ezra Pound "Canto LXXI" (from his prison
latrine and cell outside Pisa, Italy 1945)

I come to the Garden alone
in the flannelfogged morning, pass the just-
opened gates, in under beclouded trees,
into the *brouillard*, feeling strange and lost
as if I had never been here before —
as if suffocated under a vast hooded
XXXL gray chamoiscloth sweatshirt draped
over the Garden. I hear the rattling chairs,

hear the waiters flipping down the wood-slatted
seats, hear one waiter's foghorn voice, before
I can see them. The smell of coffee cuts
through the haze--the Café Millennium
is open--the waiter greets me like an old friend.

Flannel-mouthed, I drink my café au lait,
watch the ghostly fogbank advance, retreat.
Then I see a fogdog in the sky over
Notre Dame. The mist begins to dissipate.
  The Imus Crew arrives, sets up chairs and tables, cables, mikes and monitors,
cameras. Then Imus and McCord appear, check the setup, give directions,
laugh at the sign: "The I-Man at the Café Millennium--Writers Day
Paris 2000." They talk to the waiter. He walks them over to my table:
"Monsieur Stoney, I tell these gentlemen you are writer *homme de lettres aussi*
and you know the guests today--were here with them all *après-midi*
yesterday." I stand up, shake hands. "Mind if we join you?" McCord asks.
"Please do." We sit down. "So you're a writer?" Imus says with that certain
edge he has. "Yeah," I say, "and the oldest living member of the Hank
Williams Fan Club." "No way," Imus says, "I am. You can't be a bigger fan,
can't be older —" "We're the same age, exactly, almost to the day I think."
"OK," Imus says
"Tell me the flip side of 'Your Cheating Heart.'"
"That's a trick question." "Don't jump ugly with me."
"OK, Cheatin' Heart *is* the flip side. 'Lovesick Blues' was the A side."
"Label?" "M-G-M, bright yellow, not the dull off-yellow of SUN."
The quiz continues. "Who covered it--what label?" "Frankie Laine on
Columbia, red label, flip side was 'I Believe'. Joni James also on M-G-M.
Hell, man, everybody covered it. Greatest flip side in history." "Tell us some
more," McCord says. "When and where was Hank born," Imus says.
"In a two-room log cabin, outside Georgiana, Alabama near where I built a log
cabin in the woods in '62. Hank was born September 17, 1923. Father was a
dirt-poor shell-shocked World War One Vet." "Died?" "Somewhere near Oak
Hill, West Virginia, in the back seat of his Cadillac on New Year's Day 1953.
He was 29. Growing up, I felt like I was in that car with him when he died."
"Me too," Imus says, "but maybe I was driving." I can see I've passed this
part of the exam. "So what's the real deal,"Imus says, "you really in some
Hank Williams Fan Club? Why do you know all this stuff?" "Reckon you
just remember the color and smell and taste of certain life-shaping sounds,
moments," I say. McCord says: "Remember how those old 78s smelled? CDs
don't smell like anything. "Right," I say, "and no,
never been in a Hank Williams Fan Club or your Fan Club or mine or any

Fan Club." "You're a tough character aren't you," Imus says.
"No, just precise. You can't have real passion without precision."
"Oh yeah I forgot," Imus says, the edge back in his voice and eyes,
"that's what makes you a writer." The waiter brings more coffee and bottled
water. Imus looks at me, gimlet-eyed, says "Who else did you like at the same
time as Hank?" "Dostoyevsky, Hemingway, Lord Byron, Thomas Wolfe,
the usual suspects, Baudelaire, Rimbaud —" "I mean singers, man!"
"They *sang*, didn't they? Hank *wrote* didn't he?" "I mean like records
in the early 50s!"
"OK. With Hank, Fats was indispensable.
'Ain't That A Shame' and everything afterwards."
"Godamighty," Imus says. "Me too. You had to have
Hank and Fats. What's not to like about Fats."
Outside the Garden, police sirens sound
like a wailing sax under the piano-sky.
  "Who'd you like in the 60s?" McCord asks me. "Early Dylan. First few
albums and some later stuff." "And now?" "Tough question. Anybody who
brings song, story, and poetry together in a melodic instant, a rhythmic
3-minute epiphany. How about Jerry Jeff Walker. An old storytelling road-
friend who survived the 60s. Most of them didn't. He came through, with
story and style —" "Wait a minute," Imus says, "you're not this Stoney
character Jerry Jeff was talking about on my show? sings about on three or
four records?" "Reckon I am, sort of." "He'll be here tomorrow — we're doin
a Singer-Songwriter show, followup on today's writers show," McCord says,
"with Dylan and Fats and Jerry Jeff." "Why not get Hank, too, I can get him
for you," I say, "and maybe this time you'll let Jerry Jeff get past the part
where he calls me a bullshitter on National TV, let him sing 'Stoney' instead of
interrupting him, making him do 'Bo Jangles.'" "Yeah," McCord says, "all tha
magic and freedom and story-telling in that song makes me wish I was on
the road with you guys." "You know," I say, changing the subject, not wanting
to put my mouth on it, "one of the writers you've got on today's show,
Lawrence Durrell, is in the song." "I noticed that," McCord says, "what's
that all about?" "Just straight fact from the old road," I say, "funny thing is,
later I got to know Larry. Ask Durrell about it, he knows the song."
"OK," Imus says, "I will. And tomorrow Jerry Jeff sings 'Stoney'"
"Great," I say, then laugh: "And while you're at it plug my next book. Plug
some poets for a change. I never hear you mention poets — they need the plug
Poets are starving everywhere. If Hank was alive today, he'd be a starving
poet." "So you know all these writers we're interviewing today?" McCord
says. "Yeah, I'm the guy that got them here and talked them into doing the
show," I say, "and they all need their books plugged, except maybe Hemingwa

"Well, where the hell are they?" Imus says, "we're on in fifteen minutes."
"They'll be here," I say. "What's the deal with them, the inside story," McCord
says, "anything we should ask them?"
"They're all great. Immortal. Some neglected.
Some crazy." I start to warn them about Ezra
but skip it. "All of them victimized by media
in some way. So they'll be camera-shy.
Except maybe Durrell. But all real writers
are shy. Nobody's shyer than Hemingway.
It comes from living alone inside
language for so long. There's more solitude
in one sentence by these guys than most people
will ever know in a lifetime. Just let them talk."
One of the Imus crew comes over, whispers something to Imus and McCord.
They get up to leave. They both say we'll talk later. OK, I say. It's good
to talk to these guys, after hearing them on the radio for what?—twenty-some
years?—after seeing them do Radio on TV for the last how many years?
I like them both and I hope the writer's show is not a disaster, I know the
singer show tomorrow won't be, but knowing all these writers I have a
pretty good idea of what might go wrong. Scott if he's had a drink. Or
Larry and his shorts. Faulkner sitting in stony silence. Aldington if he gets
on the T.E. Lawrence thing. Ezra, for God's sake, if the wrong button is
pushed. And then, if Imus pushes that button and blows up Ezra, Papa's
wrath. But Imus and McCord can handle this if anybody can, they're good
at it. McCord is quiet, cool, very solid. Smart. Imus is smart and outrageous,
but not really as outrageous as most people think. He's — well, ask his
millions of fans what he is. Right now, all I know is we were born in the same
year, we like the same music; we both hopped freights and we were both in the
Marines. So we move in a certain mysterious synchronicity. Dylan and Jerry
Jeff, too. All of us born at the same time, loving and hating the same things on
the same clock all these years, hearing, seeing, doing many of the same things
in some of the same ways I reckon that makes synchronicity or is it
synchroneity? What was it Jung said about synchronicity as proof for the
existence of God? Anyway it isn't just contemporaneousness God knows —
plenty of contemporaries never loved and hated the same things couldn't tell the
difference between Fats and Pat Boone singing "Ain't That A Shame" never
knew what was phoney and what was real. It's not just contemporaneity. It's
complicated and it involves the probable fact that we were all pilgrim-quest-
ing-seeking-rambling-crazy, and big star or little star, we had to fight, elude,
escape the trap, wrestle the myth of the doomed singer, the doomed vagabond,
the doomed star, the doomed poet. All that Keats-in-the-streets-I'd Rather-Die-

Young-Bourbon Street syndrome. Who was it went to the top of the charts in
the 50s with "I'd Rather Die Young"? And all the girls cried. I'd rather die
Jung. Yeah right. So maybe we were all just crazy contemporary characters
doomed by myth or song or the road and we lived and lasted and kept
moving and learned to love through all that simultaneous motion and now
we want to give back that unlearnable unearnable grace, give it away in
beatitude and blessing (like Imus and his Ranch for kids and how about a
Ranch for Writers and Singers?) and since everything authentic is simulta-
neous maybe it has nothing to do with generations or when you were born
what you saw suffered sang and even if you don't like the songs they're
singing now the kids born in the 70s and 80s are moving toward, against all
the odds, the same condition of beatitude and blessing, and some will make it
to that authentic place of stillness where five thousand years, ten millenniums
of pilgrims sing so forget the easy merely generational synchroneity bit and
stop slinging your everything-but-the-kitchen-sink-chronicity and feel
compassion for those who do not have a seat at the Café Millennium (yes but
compassion erases all distinction) (no compassion doesn't do that it's mere
tenderness that does that) and remember that the Maitre D' of this Café has
an ample design

The fog, the clouds, completely gone now, the sun
dazzles the Garden, the flowers, trees and fountains.
I turn around and see Jerry Jeff and Bob Dylan and yes
Hank Williams and Fats Domino walking toward my table--
Another one of those days at the Café Millennium.

We all greet each other and sit in the silent sun.
Hank is still lean, cadaverous, gaunt, haunted,
even his eyes look lonesome under that hat
that's still too big for his head --
but he's changed somehow.
Fats looks like he did when I saw him in New Orleans
in '62. Shaking his hand makes me think
of all those long afternoons in the 50s
when my hands tried to do what his did to the piano,
to unlearn "Moonlight Sonata" and master the Domino-
poetry. He's still got that same smile, too. Fats always
makes you feel better, even when he sings loss
and shame, death, misery and the "Valley of Tears."
Dylan mumbles under some kind of hat
down low over his eyes, looking like a man

who's been born again and again and is surprised
to find he's still alive. Jerry Jeff--
well, I've seen him looking better, but hey
he's a survivor and anyway
we all looked better on the road in '63.
    Fats and Hank are saying how much they admired each other's work.
Then Dylan tells them how much he dug their songs when he was a kid,
how they sang him into being, and I'm watching Dylan turn into a kid
again, innocent, almost cherubic as he tells them what their music meant to him.
He looks like he did that night at Gerde's Folk City in the Village was it '61
or early '62 when his name was still Zimmerman and we both got our
fifteen minutes on stage on what they called Hootenanny Night. We all
thought then that he was funny on stage, clever and clownish, but it wasn't
long before we knew that he was writing and singing the songs some of us
that age were trying to write and sing but he was doing it better than any of
us. I mention that night at Gerde's and he laughs, remembering. . .Then I
tell him about that night not much later when I was in the audience and he
was on the stage alone, standing there deep inside his new-earned name, and
he sang for the first time in public his new song -- about a Hard Rain that
was a-gonna fall -- it was utterly new and very old, prophetic, ancient and
authentic, and everybody was stunned, the whole place speechless, breath-
less, frozen in a terrific silence before the standing wave of applause broke
and those of us who were singer-songwriters in the bardic mode knew right
then we might as well trash our prophetic robes and go to Nashville and
write country songs because we couldn't beat him couldn't catch him. And
nobody ever came close. "But then, too," I say, turning to Hank, "in Nash-
ville we discovered we couldn't match you. So we just drifted around the
country singing everything and anything wherever they'd listen. Hank, you
should've been there the night Bob first sang 'Hard Rain'" — Hank inter-
rupts me, says, "I love that song. They play it all the time up in heaven.
Some cat named Augustine sings a mean version of it. 'Hard Rain' and
'Gotta Serve Somebody' get as much air time up there as 'I Saw the Light'."
Hank smiles. I say to Hank:
"You sang a restless lonesome God into
our cheating hearts and Fats taught us how to sing
our way out of the shame, the blame of it all,
gave us the notes of the Fortunate Fall--
da-datta-datta-da." "No, man," Dylan says,
"It went like this: dam-dam-dam-dam-ya-ta."
    "We gonna get literary this early in the morning?" I ask. "You can't *spell*
what a piano or a guitar does anyway." "Man," Dylan says, "ain't this

Writers Day at the Café Millennium?" "Did you see," I say, "where
they're using big chunks of Eliot's 'Prufrock' in a TV commercial--for an
insurance company and they don't even acknowledge Eliot or the fact that it's
poetry. One of my neighbors thinks it's such a beautiful commercial,
she doesn't even know it's poetry, let alone Eliot. She tells me I should
write commercials like that." "I saw that," Dylan says, "the great indecision
revision indeed there will be time lines — for an insurance company you
believe that?" "How do they get away with that," Jerry Jeff says. "They'll
steal anything you don't keep your eye on," Fats says. "Maybe it's out of
copyright," Hank says. "I'll ask Ernie when I get back to the streets of
glory. He'll know. Papa's downright PO'd about all these Hemingway
Furniture commercials. You know he's a gospel singer now?" "Always
was," I say. "Papa sings bass," Hank says, "Ezra Pound sings tenor.
Anyways, funny thing, up there everybody knows Eliot was a great poet, but
all Tom does now is sing country songs. I taught him all he knows on the
guitar and gave him one of my old stage-suits and hats." The image of T.S.
Eliot in a glittery suit and cowboy hat singing "Cold Cold Heart" makes me
laugh, and Dylan, then everybody laughs. I'm remembering things like the
time we set all of "The Waste Land" to music, some rock, some folk, some
blues and country. Performed it in a coffeehouse. And remembering how
most of the professors and poets and critics were putting him down in the
60s but when he died the colleges cancelled classes and closed down for
two days in '65. And I think of neglected forgotten Kenneth Patchen dying
a few years later and nobody mentioned it. Oh Christ Christ Christ that the
world should be so dark -- Hank interrupts my meditation:
"Say, maybe you fellers know this ole boy
what just reached the streets of glory was it just
the other day--you know there ain't no day or night or time
in heaven. Feller by the name of Ginsberg.
Some kind of beatitude-poet, what they call him
up there. Down here they called him Beatnik."
    Dylan says, "Yeah I knew him." "I met him," I say, then look at Dylan:
"I just saw that documentary with you and Allen standing at Kerouac's grave
where people leave mementos all around, wine bottles and joints and beads
and candles and you were saying 'I want to be in an unmarked grave.'"
"That's right, man," Dylan says, "Allen was talking about death that day,
said he wasn't afraid of it, said he was exhilarated as he approached death
since everything he'd ever tried to say was always all about heaven." "Ain't
nothing to be scared of," Hank says. "Anyways, I'm a-tryen to teach that
Ginsberg feller to pick guitar, anything to get him offen that damned triangle
thing he makes a racket with, scarifying all the angels, beating on it

the livelong day." Jerry Jeff and I look at each other, as if to say you hearing this, you digging this too? and we ain't scared either, are we? Fats asks Hank about his grandmother and Hank rests his hand hieratically on Fats' shoulder and says she's getting along just fine. "She was cooking up a storm at a church supper with my mama not long ago. Up there, we all know most everybody and everybody gets along fine. It's hard to put your mouth on it down here but it's like that love we was always trying to sing about really does exist like it's what you breathe and move in every day and there ain't no more lonesomeness no more a-cryen--at first that was the only hard part for me, getting through the day without being sad and lonesome and restless. . ." We all say nothing and listen to the backbeat rhythm of the fountains and watch the Imus Show getting ready to go on the air. And I'm thinking if you could just bring all the generations of writers and singers together, the entire century, the whole millennium of poets and singers together, maybe you could bring everything to the edge of epiphany why just the edge well I reckon you can't write or sing much closer than the edge of Epiphany because the rest is up to —
Then Buddy Holly and the Big Bopper walk
through the Garden, harmonizing and laughing.
"Part of me died that day," Dylan says.
"Me too," I say in unison with Jerry Jeff.
Then we see, down by the sunblazoned fountain,
Buddy and the Big Bopper talking to Leadbelly,
Blind Lemon and Woody, and Piaf flirting
with Baudelaire, and Izaak Walton watching
Satchmo blow an ethereal horn making fish
leap in the fountain, and Kerouac seems
to be arguing with Walt Whitman -- it looks like
they're talking loud, intense, gesturing with hands
and arms, but we can't hear what they say.
    "Did you see on that film," Dylan says, "when Kerouac was on the William Buckley Show talking about how people don't understand what the so-called Beats were about. And Buckley asks Jack if he is a Hippie and Jack looks mad and says he is *not* a so-called Hippie. Then he looks Buckley in the eye and says
'I believe in order, tenderness, and piety.'"
    "I saw it," I say, "they should play it everyday in literature and writing classes, at poetry slams, in shopping malls." "Yeah, man, order, tenderness, and piety. That's what it was always about somehow." "Maybe you always knew that. I learned it somewhere on the road. All of us who were really there knew about tenderness, we'd had our epiphanies, dazed on the road to Damascus or New Orleans by a vision of tenderness, a great wave of compassion,

an oceanic sense of brotherhood and sisterhood that was maybe a little too oceanic. I mean we were in danger for a while there of confusing abstract sinister tenderness with real compassion, like Flannery O'Connor says — the sin of the modern world." "Yeah, that too. And we believed in order and piety all along but we had to find a new way to talk about it." "I reckon we knew all along that we had to rediscover or reinvent or reclaim the order and piety that we had lost, or never had, or had taken away from us." "We knew that, but sometimes with too much pride and arrogance. And self-righteousness. But compassion, when it really takes you, erases all of that." "That's why we admired the old people who were wise and had stories to tell, the people who had really lived and lasted." "With dignity. And stories." "With order, tenderness, and piety, like old Jack said. Not that later 60s formula of disorder, selective tenderness, and mockery." "Chaos, insiderness, blasphemy." "The recent ruling class values." "That wasn't Beat, that was the phoney- hippie-solipsist-anarchist-in-love-with-death movement stuff." "The New York times says the two myths of the 60s were the myth of cultural liberation through 'libidinal ecstasy and fabulous excess' and the myth of a 'morally righteous generation rising up against war, racism, and materialism' says that —" "What's this-shere New York Times fellers," Hank says, "we don't get that delivered in heaven." "I'm not surprised." "It's a paper and just last week they said that the 60s are now seen as either a time of dangerous utopianism that was really totalitarian delusion or a time of moral purity unknown to today's era of rampant materialism and cynicism. They don't get it." "All Golden Age Myths are insidious." "The 50s were the Golden Age, man, not the 60s. The good stuff in the 60s was born in the 50s." "Maybe it just feels that way because we were kids in the 50s, almost innocent, or because Fats and Hank sang the 50s, or because —" "The late 60s turned our songs inside out —" "Woodstock was Kerouac's worst nightmare come true —" "Maybe that's why he died in '69 —"
"Say now," Hank says, "you fellers ain't Beatniks are you?"
"They called us that when we were kids," Dylan says.
"Called me that when I was 16," I say.
"I don't see how you could be living
inside my music," Hank says, "and Fats' music
and be a Beatnik." "We had the beat," Fats says.
"Just a label they used," I say. "Sure
we were after Beatitude,
blessing the world and being blessed by it.
Just like you. So you'all were Beatniks too.
Screw labels. I was just a kid in love
with the road, with distance, motion, trying

to see some country, sing some country,
trying to be free the only way I knew
how then, to sing being free on the road."
   "But sometimes we got confused about what freedom really is, didn't we?"
"Ain't nobody ever kept that particular item straight for very long." All
the time we're talking i'm hearing songs inside my head yes it's me ooo-wee
baby i'm in love again on blueberry hill i'm so lonesome i could cry don't
think twice in the hard rain we were that free then walkin' down the road
hearing the songs feeling them bring back the way only songs can how things
were, how they looked and felt and smelled and tasted a long long time ago
(that feels like now when you sing the song) and i don't really listen to the talk
anymore because i'm hearing all the songs kept you goin' when the road got
rough mister bojangles dance cold cold cheating heart you win again ain't
that a shame calling you in the valley of tears midnight slow train gotta serve
somebody crazy little mama come knock-knock-knocking at heaven's door i
saw the light ooo-oo-wee and hearing all the songs and watching Aldington
Durrell Faulkner Fitzgerald Hemingway and Pound walk toward me through
the Garden and Imus and McCord run over to say they're on the air in two
minutes i'm thinking why is it the writers i love have lousy taste in music i
know the songs they know and don't know: the songs they could have heard
but didn't hear — is it that poetry runs ahead of song or the other way around
or maybe writers can't sing and singers can't write yeah right and i'm introdu-
cing the writers to the singers telling Faulkner that Hank's the man who wrote
Cheatin' Heart and Faulkner stares and has obviously never heard of it and
Hank says "And what do you do, Mr. Faulkner?" (and an image flashes of
Faulkner writing *A Fable* at the very moment that Cheatin' Heart is the num-
ber one song in the world but Faulkner is grooving on Lawrence Welk or
singing along with Rudy Vallee) and i know it's going to be a long day at the
Café Millennium as the writers go over to start the show but it's OK every
thing authentic every thing real that matters, is simultaneous, and anything
can happen at this Café, has already happened, will keep happening and since
everything is continuous this is (to be continued. . .)

Stay tuned —
Watch your millennial TV Guide for dates
and times of broadcast. With Dylan and Fats
and Hank and Jerry Jeff I watched Imus
and McCord interview the famous writers.
   You had to be there. Then the next day Imus had all of us on the air, talking,
singing together, Dylan, Fats and Hank, the famous writers chanting their
great lines, Imus asking Jerry Jeff and me about being on the road in the early

60s, Ezra and Faulkner talking about walking through Europe in the 20s. Ezra and Papa sang along with Fats and Hank. You had to be there.

Imus announced plans to have Derek Walcott, Lord Byron, Milan Kundera and Goethe on the next show, together with Jimmy Rodgers the Yodeling Brakman, Enrico Caruso and Hank Locklin. And Dolly Parton would sing a duet with John Milton. Imus wanted to do a painters show, too — asked me to help him get Cézanne, Picasso, Warhol, and Michelangelo. And I helped him set up a show with Saint Jack Kerouac and Ginsberg, T.S. Eliot and Flannery O'Connor, Kitty Wells, Jenny Lind and Adrienne Rich. Bernie said he'd try to get Gertrude Steinem. I missed these shows because I hit the road again with Jerry Jeff. Ezra, Faulkner, Hank, and Hemingway came with us, walking deep into France by way of Mississippi. Ezra got lost somewhere. In any case, it is hoped that transcripts of these extraordinary broadcasts will soon be approved for release. Videos of these programs may be available soon at your local millennial video store. Maybe not. Do not contact Imus regarding these shows or he will certainly push that button. You know the one.

Stay tuned —
this is what we are after:
singers and writers together
chanting the ethereal harmonies of the empyrean:
precision and passion, exactitude and amplitude,
beatitude and blessing
in the deep simultaneity
of story and song that connects, transcends,
redeems mere generational synchronicities --

Stay tuned
the Café Millennium is always open

Heat Wave: Or, Through the Millennial Car-Wash with Saint Augustine

I was sitting at the Dodge dealership, in the hot garage,
Waiting for my truck to be serviced,
Fearing the estimate for air-conditioning
Repairs in the middle of a Heat Wave.
I was thinking, while I was talking
To the service manager about dyes and leaks
And evaporators, about Saint Augustine,
How he said we would outgrow our carnal sins
And all the rest he had to say about Staying Cool.

Then my truck was ready. The AC estimate was high
So I went for two pounds of Freon to get me through
The Heat Wave. I paid, went outside, and there's Saint
Augustine in my truck, fiddling with the AC controls.
"It works perfectly, man," he said, as if we're old
Friends. I stay cool, start it up: "Where do you want
To go?" I ask as he rattles on about the truck of the year,
About how he loves Dodge trucks, especially 4x4's.
Then he said: "Let's go to the Car Wash."

I figured I'd take the old guy wherever he wanted
To go--as Saints go, he's a good one, and I liked
The way he rode shotgun, the way he liked my truck,
The way he sang along with my Piaf tape, raucous,
Loud: "Non! Rien de rien. Non! Je ne regrette rien. . ."
When Piaf is through, he sings it again in Latin.
Then he says: "Is St. John of the Cross her songwriter?"
We both laugh. I park in front of the video store;
We go inside to return a movie. In the war section

We walk past Saint Thomas Aquinas, stuffing his face
With potato chips. He's looking at the box for "Saving
Private Ryan." Augustine nods, but he doesn't speak,
Mutters "Just War" under his breath as we head
To the Foreign Film section. He says: "Get 'Manon
Of the Springs', anything with water in it for later."
We check out, go back to the truck. He's quiet, he

Studies the mall, the stores, reads all the signs,
Notes the way people move in the infernal heat.

Stopped at a red light, he gives me this serious look,
Says: "I've been watching TV, reading the newspapers,
All this silly Millennial talk. And professors, too,
Talking about the Death of History as the single
Great fact of the next Millennium. Of course the Past
Is Dead. They killed it two hundred years ago."
"Yeah right," I say. "The Past is Dead and the Future
Ain't what it used to be." He laughs: "They killed
It long ago. It's tragic, but it's old news." The light

Changed. "And you've paid the price of that death. Look
At this Century." I looked at it. He apologizes
For being serious, then says: "Let me tell you the real
Millennial News: the Death of Sex, not the Death of History.
Sex will end in Y2K. There won't be any more
Except under necessary laboratory conditions.
And that's not sex. And what your computer Future
Prophets say, about a bodily and mental Internet,
So you can enter others, know union, have sex

Through the computerized access built into your cells —
Well, dear brother, that ain't sex is it?"
We stopped at another red light. "If it is
It ain't what it used to be." "Right on, brother,"
He says. "Sex will end. *Securus iudicat orbis terrarum.*
The Verdict" — I interrupted his translation:
"Yeah I know, the world's verdict is conclusive."
"*Roma locuta est,*" he laughs, "and it ain't just Rome
That has spoken. The world will be better off

Without sex, the source of all crime, murder, mayhem,
War, just about everything. Not to mention sin.
And you can save a few bucks on your air-conditioning."
He starts singing: "*Da mihi castitatem et continentiam,
Sed noli modo. . .*" I harmonize in English (to the tune
Of "The Bells Are Ringing") "Oh give me chastity
And give me continence, But please do not give it to me

Just yet. . ." The light changed. We drove into the Car Wash.
"Why don't you call me Augie," he says. "Or you can call me Gus."

He looks excited as we approach the dark tunnel. He reads
The choices aloud: "Rust Inhibitor. Polish and Wax. Sealer
Wax. Under-Carriage Wash. Grand Slam. We must have the Grand
Slam!" The attendant comes to the window. "Grand Slam,"
I say, handing him a ten. Augie leans over, hands the kid
A five, says "My name's Gus. Here's a little extra
For letting us stay in there longer." "Neutral. No brakes,"
The kid says thanking us, giving Saint Augustine a weird
Look. And then we go into the waterfall, three-inch blue

Belts slapping the truck on top, on the sides, behind,
Vision obscured by the foamy waves. "Do you feel that?"
Augie says, "that slow sexy rhythm, vibration and Oh
The waterfall." I listened and tried, just for Gus,
To feel everything that was happening. The truck moved.
Augie flattened his hands against the windshield, as if
Trying to swim through, or hold back, the waterfall,
A look of child-like radiance on his face. Water came down
In heavy waves, the blue belts slapping furiously.

"And now we're a submarine," Gus says, "being swallowed
By a Giant Blue Octopus." "Also known as Devilfish," I note.
"Don't be pedantic," Gus says and we move through the dark
Tunnel in silence, surface by the flashing lights and he reads
"Rust Inhibitor Now Being Applied." "Sealer Wax Now Being Applied"
He sings as if chanting a sacred text "Under-Carriage Wash
Now Being Applied — OH YES so clean and cool all the burning
Gone in one Grand Slam. Yes Ma'm!" We emerged, thrust
Bright and shining into the sun. Gus said nothing.

I shifted out of neutral, eased over to the coin vacuum
Machine. As I get out to vacuum, Gus looks pensive, says
"Ah if only they'd had Chariot-Washes when I was young."
I open the back of the truck, clean the fishing trip mattress,
Get all the spilled bait and topsoil and mulch. I come back
To the cab, St. Augustine's gone. The note on the dashboard

In a neat hand: "Since sex will end next year, shouldn't
We get a Car-Wash franchise--nationwide, hell worldwide chain?"
The note was signed: "Stay Cool. Your buddy, Augustine."

"Signs of the Times: Y2K"

I saw the first sign at the Mall:
"Y2K--1-800-Red-Alert!"
Wrote the number down, wondering
If this was about a new Red Scare,
Or some religious message, some special software.
When I called the number I learned
That, for a hefty fee, I could attend
(With my "loved ones" — all family members free)
A Seminar that would prepare
Us for the coming catastrophe.

I began to notice the signs everywhere (Call BUG-2000),
Grocery stores (Call 800-END-TIME), telephone poles.
Y2K is coming, and we are not ready:
Utilities, infrastructure, all systems will fail.
The banks will close, the planes will crash,
Credit will be cut off, and we'll have no cash.
A French friend called from Paris,
Profoundly concerned about "Le Bug" (luh boog)
That could not be fixed. Usually calm, lucid,
He was very upset that he could not fly

To New York for New Year's Day, Y2K.
I told him to come on Christmas and stay
Until they fixed it. He said that would do
No good. He saw a sign in the Metro,
Called the number, and was told that Christ
Was coming again on that last Christmas,
The world would end in millennial fire
Before the computers crashed.
"We won't even get to Y2K!"
He plans to watch the end from a café in St.-Tropez.

At the supermarket I saw the sign: "1-Y2K-RAP-TURE."
Teenagers were reading it, too. One said:
"Awesome dude, a millennial rap-tour."
I called that number. An alto voice, very breathy,
Somehow very sexy,

Told me about the end-time, the Rapture,
Either next Christmas or New Year's —
She was not sure which day the Christ-Fire would take us —
But I must join her in prayer to prepare.
I was struck by the sound/subject disparity,

The way she breathed those singular words
Into the phone. I do not know how phonesex
Is supposed to sound but this, to be sure,
Was some deep form of telerapture.
I called other numbers on other signs.
I pondered the dilemma.
The time to act, quite clearly, was now:
December, unseasonably warm, actually hot,
Some millennial El Nino, some vast apocalyptic
Greenhouse closing down around my garden.

With the entire country on a runaway train,
Riding a oneway ticket to Paula Jonestown,
I turned off CNN, C-SPAN, killed the television, went outside,
Tore up, scattered in mulch piles, my notes on all the signs.
In the warm December dirt, I knelt down
In my garden, remulched next summer's garlic crop,
Burying deep the sweet green sprouts; then scooped
Mulch close and firm around my Advent-fattening leeks,
The poireaux we will eat in April (every April).
Hammered deeper my signs: 12 kinds of leek, 12 kinds of garlic.

Then I felt ready, ready for Christmas,
Ready for any calendrical conundrum,
Ready for Big Mama Millennium.
Just to be certain, I planted a penny, heads up,
(Oh the banks will all crash and we'll have no cash)
Under the scarecrow of the old century,
Under the dying fall of the last chrysanthemum
Bloom of the ancient weary millennium.
Before darkness took the Decemberslanting sun, preparing for Y2K,
I made a few new signs for my garden hideaway.

Bacillus Thuringiensis: Or, Frankenfood and Frankenpoems

No, this is not your local Luddite gardener
Speaking, with dire warnings about genetically
Altered food. I am not your neighborhood
Enviroalarmist prophesying wastelands,
Denouncing bovine growth hormones,
Phoney potatoes,
Fake tomatoes,
Forlorn corn,
Infected forever with their own
Insecticides. From the labs that gave us
Agent Orange. Now, in agribusiness
Avatar, they pose as prophets of the earth.
They play with ruining everything forever.
(And you *should* pay attention to the Bt
In your BLT, and where you buy your corn.
The safest thing is to grow your own.)
But of course you know all about Frankenfood —
Bacillus Thuringiensis — and how
It hassles us, this whoring menace
To the Great Chain of Being and Growing.

I do wish to warn you of a new threat,
Revealed here for the first time: Sinister
Plots are afoot to create Frankenpoems,
To alter the genes of poets, imprint
Insceticides, for example, that kill
Free verse, inject iambicides that permit poets
To write only Dactylic Tetrameter trots.
Or equally sinister, all rhyme will wither,
Rhythm and meter will die like beetles,
And all words of more than one syllable,
All words that do not end in -uck,
All words requiring use of a dictionary,
Will be no more than memories in the Burpee
Poemseed Catalog.
It may not be long before admission
To Creative Writing Programs requires
A shot of bacillus thuringiensis

Or its poetry counterpart Gbg
(Also known as gaseous boring-genesis).
I am neither Tiresias nor Tacitus
Come to warn you about this bacillus —
But I do have connections in the CIA,
The Central Insecticide Agency.
            il faut resister must be our motto
            like French farmers storming MacDonald's
            yet for all we know the ecopoeticosystem
            may already be doomed to Frankenpoems
            the poemicide bacteria already
            in our anthologies
            in our tomatoes, our corn, in every bite:

            datta   damyata   dna
            shantih   A&P   Shop-Rite

"'The Times They Are A-Changing' -- But No No No It Aint Me I Aint Changing No More"
(Or Automatic Writing Instantaneously Transcribed By Aging Singer-Songwriter Upon Striking A Certain Guitar Chord)

Come gather round people where ever you roam —
Oh we sang it on the road, we sang it at home
In a thousand clubs marches rallies coffeehouses jukejoints
And always, when we sang it, they knew we meant it and took
It personally: You better start swimming or you'll sink like a stone
Oh yes we sang it and we made revolution
More sure of the song than any solution
For the Times they are a-cha-a-a-angin
We sang for Civil Rights, we sang for Freedom,
We sang against the War, we sang the cities into flames
We sang Love and Peace and Brotherhood until all the others —
The chorus, a few years younger, singing along with us —
Turned love into hate, peace into rage
Brotherhood and Sisterhood into race and gender wars
The line it is drawn the curse it is cast

      Harsh, angry, driven, we sang it all together
      Then Jay went to Vietnam and flew two hundred
      Bombing runs and was never the same again
      And John got fragged by a grenade outside Saigon
      And Jake died stoned in a motorcycle crash at 120 MPH
      And Joe made love not war and died of a drug overdose
      And Janice had six abortions before she killed herself
      And Jim went to Wall Street and became a billionaire
      And Jack and Jill went over the hill and were never seen again
      (Though they are rumored to be teaching Freshman Composition
      Or peddling Deconstruction) Some survived Ph.D.'s
      Some survived the Marines and kept singing as long as they could
      Never betraying the Sacred Circle, the Kunderesque-dance
      The handheld passion of "We Shall Overcome" Never confessing
      Complicity in what went wrong But refusing the copout: —
                          "It was just a song"

The Order is rapidly fading and it did and it still fades
In the dying fall of the song in supermarket aisles, music
To shop by, it must sound as old to our children (and grandchildren)
As Aint She Sweet & other Roaring Twenties songs sounded to us in the 60s —
Come Mothers and Fathers throughout the land And don't criticize
What you can't understand Oh we understand all right, and our parents
Understood even as we denied them thrice and didn't think twice
And kept on singing and our rapt robotic audience kept on dancing
The vast mad arrogant spitting-on-cops-and-soldiers Closed Circle Dance
Of 1968 and after: Then we stopped singing.
Yet still, a lifetime later, on a certain summer night, we might
Sing the song with all the old feeling, passion, hope, still feel
That mad rage for change tinged with a sense of immeasurable loss.
And when the song has faded into the edges of night "WHAT WENT
WRONG?" echoes like a great accusing question we cannot answer,
Cannot even sing.

Some days now we dream of giving all our songs and labor,
All our money to some Universal Bureau of Expiation;
Of calling old Bobby, Kid Zimmy, who grew up like us,
Devouring and devoured by the same songs and visions,
Hank & Fats & Early Elvis Buddy Woody, making the same songs
On the same stages, calling him to say Hey Mr. Tambourine Man
Cough it up Mr. Rollingstone, give all your money to the truly poor,
The war-scarred exiles, the bankrupt farmers For the Times A-a-rrre
A-Cha-a-a-ngin But No, No, No, it aint me, I aint changing no more
For the hard rain fell and we were the rainmakers
And only those who led the singing truly know the score
And there aren't many of us around anymore (we were never many)
And all we have left from those old days, one thing we're sure of —
(Aside from a haunting intricate shadowy shifting Sense of Betrayal) —
We truly were, and truly made, the Times we sang, and singing,
changed.

"Was it just a song?"

Lecture on Walls and Stones

(A Spontaneous Lecture delivered upon finding a forgotten
piece of the Berlin Wall in the cluttered drawer of my typing desk)

I have here in my hand a piece of the Berlin Wall.
The first time I saw the Wall, long ago, I was in Berlin
To do a live country music concert on the British Radio
Network. Pretty strange, huh? — how the MC and the Cultural
Attache seemed to think that Hank Williams and Johnny Cash
Would be useful in cheering up the troops,
In subverting the East, undermining the Commy Regime.
Later, when we went through the Wall at Checkpoint Charlie,
She, the Cultural Attache, said something about Good Fences
Make Good Neighbors. I said "Something there is that loves
A Wall" but she didn't get it and I wasn't really thinking
About Robert Frost--I kept thinking how Checkpoint Charlie
Sounded like the name of some country singer I couldn't remember,
Singing about the wings of an eagle, and flying over prison walls.
All those border crossings, like all walks on the dangerous edge
Of things, made you feel utterly alive and free,
Like singing, like poetry,
Like a kid walking, balancing, on a wall
Or silently skipping stones across wide water.

The last time I saw the Wall I was on the train
From Leningrad, where we did a folk-country concert on the Fourth
Of July, 1984. Pretty funny, huh? — and strange also how the Wall,
Years after the first time, still reverberated with country music.
Anyway, in Leningrad, we sang at the Consul General's Mansion,
Where we also slept — get this — in the Nixon Bedroom where the walls,
The bathroom, and the vast Czarist bed were all bugged so we whispered
The important things over running water and flushing toilets.
At our concert, when I invited them, loads of Leningrad dignitaries
And Soviet Commissars joined in, sang along especially on "This Land
Is Your Land." It was funny there with the Party Chief, some KGB-types,
The Mayor and this heavy-duty bruiser named Boris joining us on stage,
Singing "Your Cheating Heart." Then Boris wanted to sing "Four Walls" —
It was not a song we usually did, but I played it for him and Boris sang

"Four Walls to hear me. . .Clo-o-singg in on me." Later, over vodka
And caviar Boris told me they always sang "This Land" and "If I Had a Ham-
mer" at Communist Youth Camps, but they liked Hank Williams and Country
better. Then the Mayor of Leningrad toasted us, asked us to return
To his great city and sing again. I said: "Thank you very much. We will

Return when Leningrad is once again —" and I stopped, seeing the worried
Americans, the State Department types, knowing I should be diplomatic.
But the Mayor finished my sentence: "When Leningrad is once again
St. Petersburg — and very soon now you will come back and sing."
So we took the Leningrad Express through Warsaw, where freedom was in
The air, into East Germany where the Customs searches were teutonically
Meticulous. We had a lot of baggage because we had been living in China,
And traveling on the Trans-Siberian Express. In Moscow I had offered
To smuggle out Samizdat manuscripts of anti-Party poetry. I was glad
They'd changed the route, didn't need my services, when the toothy East
German police dogs and snarling soldiers sniffed and searched our stuff.
When they finally left I heard, for the very first time, filling the train,
Bruce Springsteen singing "Born in the USA." I stepped out
Of the compartment; at the far end of the corridor I saw
An American singing along with the music from his boombox at the top
Of his voice: "Born in the USA!" He saw me and gave me a raised-fist
Salute. I returned it. When the soldiers moved to the next car,
I walked down to hear the music better and talk to the only other
American on the train. He was a poet, some big West Coast literary Honcho,

And I liked him right away. He had been in East Germany for a year.
He rewound, played the song again, volume all the way up. We sang.
We could hear the soldiers walking on the roof of the car.
Then we started, eased past the Berlin Wall. It was the best place,
The best way, to hear that song for the first time. The West Coast poet
Lit up as soon as we passed the Wall, leaned out the window,
Got very stoned. And kept singing all the way to France.
Years later, that first night when the world was singing and dancing
On the Wall, and tearing it down, he called from New York to say
We had to leave right away--he had tickets on the next plane to Berlin.
I couldn't go — had to teach and give exams and work on my garden fence.
I could say he brought me this piece of the Wall, but no, truth is
I bought it at some tacky discount store, clearance sale two years later,
When everybody had forgotten about the Wall. Except the Club I heard about

Where a great chunk of the Wall is installed on stage. Rock groups
And groupies dance around it, oblivious. Since the Club is called The Wall
They think it's part of the scene, the decor. Like Freshman students who,
When I mention the Wall, look blank. Then there's that Corporate Headqtrs
That has a huge piece of the Wall in a fountain in the company caféteria.

Like many people, like espionage-types
And old Cold-Warriors and career diplomats now rudderless,
Like writers of spy-thrillers
And maybe some poets and even some ordinary people,
Sometimes I miss the Wall.
It provided such a clean shape to things, definition.
I mean, without the Wall, I wouldn't have had ridiculous
KGB-guys following me around Moscow and Leningrad because
They knew I'd made contact with underground poets.
Maybe we should build a Wall in Hackensack or Keokuk,
In Vegas, or Orlando, so we can smuggle underground poetry
Across the Wall. Walls seem to increase the importance of poetry.
Like that KGB agent who followed me all day, all night, and into
That hotel bar in Leningrad. He was not ridiculous, just doing his job.
I bought him a drink and we talked, in a far dark corner of the bar,
About Walls and Poetry. He warned me about smuggling Samizdat — he
Would not arrest me, he liked poetry, but the others would. "Besides,"
He said, "for every wall we tear down we build another with the very same
Stones, rearranged. When we have more belief than truth, we build
Without poems."

The New York Times tells me that upscale young Germans are now
Gentrifying crumbling neighborhoods close to the remains of the Wall,
That they are feeling the "psychic pull of. . .the swiftly fading
Physical past." Sometimes when I make repairs on my 200-year-old
Stone wall in upstate New York, shifting massive winter-heaved stones,
Or replacing stones stolen by yuppies — (You know, don't you, that
The hottest status symbol right now is a stone wall? They're paying $100
A foot and more to build them around their country places) — I post my wall
But it does no good unless I catch them. Sometimes when I fix my wall
I think of the Berlin Wall, now part of the discarded past, as ancient
As the Pyramids. Other times, when the tire on my wheelbarrow overloaded
With stones goes flat, I think of my old buddy, a country singer, who
Sold millions of records and got rich singing "Up Against the Wall,

Redneck Mother." And I think of the KGB-tail, my friend who warned me
Long ago in that Leningrad bar. "Here, we had too much belief," he said,
"So we built walls to keep out truth." He seemed very sad, so I bought
Him another drink. "Now we have nothing. But in the scale of things,
If we were too heavy with belief, you are too heavy with freedom. Without
Concrete images of these things, that is without poetry, we have nothing."

"Perhaps we must think of ourselves as the Wall," he said, tossing off
His vodka. "Or we are the old horse, cold in the pasture, grazing toward
The Wall in the hard rain, grazing along the Wall, then turning away,
Our backs to the wind and the Wall. We do not have to apologize for the
Manner in which we graze." "So, what is the weather forecast?" I asked
Cryptically. "Partly cloudy," he said enigmatically, "but it is the other part
That troubles me." "The rain falls the same on both sides of the Wall,"
I said. "Yes," he said, ordering another round, "but the rain does not
Acknowledge the Wall, nor does the sharp-eyed soaring red-tailed hawk."
"But the hawk must land sometime," I said, touching his glass. "And who
Knows, who says the hawk cannot perch on the wall and hunt both sides?"
We were probably both drunk, whispering such wisdom as he gestured
With his eyes at the bartender and the listening walls and light fixtures.
He went over to the jukebox, played Johnny Cash — "If they freed me from
This prison, If that railroad train was mine. . ." When we left, he warned
Me in the street, firmly, not to carry any poetry across the border.
They were watching me. "And the only good wall," he said, "is a poetry wall."
The next morning, the CIA-man at the Consulate also warned me about
Samizdat, but his main concern was not poetry, just the possibility
Of an awkward incident.

The lecture is over. I do not have time this evening to wonder whether
The KGB-poet is now in Brooklyn or LA, a gangster maybe, a priest maybe,
Or writing poetry in a log-cabin somewhere in the Far West of Siberia.
And Oh Yes — Did I tell you I also have a piece of the Great Wall of China?
Which I forgot to bring tonight. That wall, dear to the hearts of tourists,
Is still standing. Very much. Oh I know that Wall well, have walked on it
Alone at sunrise and sundown. My wife got a piece of that Wall for a Nun
In New York who collects sacred stones, numinous stones of history. That
Very night, everybody in Beijing seemed to know that she had taken a piece
Of the Great Wall, as if in some primordial American Agression overheard
By all the wired walls. I picked up my piece of the Great Wall later, at a
Clandestine Easter Sunrise service high on the Great Wall, organized —
In 1984 this is — by secret Christians from the Soviet, Czech, and Polish

Embassies and Chinese underground Christians including the Poet-Priest
Whose throat had been slit *twice* by Red Guards for saying the words
Of the Mass. Counter-revolutionary espionage. Thank you very much,
Ladies and Gentlemen. That will be all for this lecture. I will bring
The stone from the Great Wall next time. However, even if I forget to tell
You all about that, remember that you will be responsible for all walls,
All stones on the Final Exam. You will be responsible for everything
On the Final Exam.

The Track of Totality

I met a New Age Druid on the road
To the Total Eclipse, bound for Cornwall.
This was the real thing, not the Millennium,
He said. He seemed to think the world would end
And he seemed rather pleased with the thought.

I bought him a cup of coffee. He told
Me about his connections with various
Groups, the Cornish Eclipse Stoneman Pagans,
And Moonshadow Rising, the New Age Travelers
Who danced Everything into Nothing.

He belonged to many earth-mystery cults,
Had been confirmed by druids at Stonehenge,
Had been arrested for uprooting crops
That had been genetically altered,
Had founded the Vegetable Anarchists.

He believed you should pay for nothing, steal
Everything, but he let me pay for the coffee.
What he wanted me to understand the most
Was the 70-mile-wide Track of Totality,
The Eclipse that would cross mystic Cornwall

At eleven past eleven on the
Eleventh day of the month — the Old World
Would die. There was nothing new in all this,
Of course. In '27, the last total eclipse
In Britain, even businessmen were mystics.
Even Virginia Woolf took the excursion

Train to the Yorkshire moors, wrote in her diary:
"We had seen the world dead." My New Age Druid
Scoffed at this. I did not understand, he said.
"This Track of Totality crosses Cornwall!
Center of all earth magic and mystery!"

I talked of the friend, a DNA research
Specialist, who planned to fly the Concorde
Eclipse Charter, paying $2,500
To ride the Midnight Special high above
The Atlantic so he could see the Black Sun

For six minutes, four more than the earthly two.
"Supernatural Supersonic," my druid
Friend said. "Suprachthonic," I added.
"Yes, and then he'll be and all will be dead,"
The wizard said sagely, ecstatically.

He seemed to think that everything would die
And he'd be left alive to survey the scene.
Now that the Track of Totality has come
And gone, and everything remains the same,
I wonder what the lab researcher

Is doing — back in the Lab making Change?
And the New Age Druid seeker, where is he?
In a Pub somewhere, watching TV?
Back in College, studying Business, Science?
Or lost in California, playing Video Games?

Peacekeeper on the Bridge

He stands on the bridge in Kosovo above
The Ibar River which divides the Serb
And Albanian sides of the town. Crowds curse,
Swarm, shove, throw things, make obscene gestures,
Murder in their eyes. They want to rape the women,
Kidnap the children, burn the houses of the Other
Side. They turn their tribal hatred against
The young French soldier keeping peace on the bridge.

He thinks of the bridges of home, on the Rhône,
At Pont-St.-Espirit, Holy Spirit Bridge,
Built by the Brotherhood of the Holy
Spirit bridgebuilders in the thirteenth century.
He smiles and thinks he's a member of that Order
Now. Then he thinks of a bridge in the Gorge
Of the Tarn. A rock hits his eye, the mob swarms,
He holds them back. There is gunfire in the hills beyond

The river. Albanians curse and chant "French
Terrorists!" making filthy signs, kicking
Him below the belt. He swoons an instant,
His finger goes to the trigger, it would be easy
To open fire on these holy war savages.
They retreat. He stands with dignity
As a rotten tomato splatters his uniform.
He thinks of the bridges of home.

    It is not easy being a peacekeeper
    On the bridge when both sides want to kill each other
    And you. So you think of the Holy Spirit
    Bridge. You know these people are in Love with Death
    And wonder if you should give them what they want.
    But you smile, remembering the bridges of home.

The Great Change Coming?

For half-a-century we've watched them, small planes
Flying low over the beaches of the Jersey Shore
Trailing their banners, advertising local bars, restaurants,
Place-pennons, soaring enduring stronghold of the local.

1999 — I run into the surf, dive under a wave
Come up feeling exactly as I did in 1950
See the low-flying plane and its banner:
"The Great Change is Coming!"

Those words sail like great clouds across the sky.
I wait for the next plane to come. It never arrives
To explicate the mysterious message. All afternoon,
Imperial emptiness rules the serene empyrean

Above the unchanging evershifting waves, my beaches
Disappearing into the sea. Somewhere the beaches must
Be getting bigger. At sundown, the band in the bar behind
The boardwalk rocks, shouts: "Bye Bye Miss Millennium Pie!"

Keep the Change

At the French village farmer's market
She holds out the rosy-golden apples
Toward me, praising their mystery and texture.
Her golden hair spills wildly from the inverted
Chalice of her stylish peasant straw-hat,
Her golden Camargue cross half-obscured
By the blue worker's apron that slices
Across amplitude of country cleavage.
She smiles a smile beyond all appling
As she thrusts the lustrous orbs in my hands:
"These apples are changing as we hold them.
They are perfect now. You must eat them soon,
Before they change." I buy seven rosy-gleaming
Apples. She wraps them lovingly, with delicate
Exactitude. She names the price. I give
Her five francs extra, saying "Keep the Change."
Then I hand one exact apple back to her.
She smiles applerapt smile from somewhere East of Eden.

I ate the apples that night with friends,
Golden sundown on the Mediterranean.
As apples know their appleness
And contemplate the ripeness toward which they yearn,
We must shun false notions of becoming,
Must scorn pernicious fantasies of change,
Insidious myths of self and progress:
When we know who we are, and what we have to give,
And how to love,
We only change by giving what we have become,
Giving freely, fully, away and away
In selfless Love from the spring of plenitude.
(Lady Brett does not get it, but the Count knows).
Like the ancient Apple Tree, in dreams of falling
In a winter storm, or stoic under April's chainsaw,
We praise our destiny, bright Christmas blaze —
Oh Keep the Change, feed the cleansing fire —
Give the Apple away, in time, beyond time.

Island Changes: Or, Islomorphic Theophanies
(for Derek Walcott)

Islands, as they float in our dreams,
Are the essence of change.
Change with precise knowable outlines,
Change with limits, disciplined by exact
Coastlines, shapes of singular waves,
Strict codes of sun, sand, and beach cafés.
The chosen island must not be too large,
Must be of a walkable finitude,
Must not promise vague continental drift-change.

Islands, as they shimmer in our visions
Of innocence, are quintessence of change.
Twelve years old, you stand on the filthy riverbank,
In any befouled city sprawled on a toxic river anywhere,
And you stare at the green shape of the midriver island.
You know if you can just get there, things will be different.
Maybe like Huck Finn, maybe on a raft you build,
Maybe it will sink, you or your friend will drown:
But the island is freedom, transformation.

Islands, as they dance in our desire, declare
No man is an island, but all men are islandesque.
Much older now, you study the Sunday Times travel pages,
Vast inventory of islomania, homilies on heliophilic
Transmutation. Then you sit in a palm-thatched café
On the beach. She says: "You change islands like changing
Partners, always looking for the perfect dance."
You say: "Islands change you even as they change,
Intricate coastal shifts in concert with the sea."

Islands, as they whisper west of the Hesperides,
Promise blessedness. Heracles, glib and glutted
With golden apples, now runs the Tourist Office.
The singing sisters, the nymphs, are loungesingers
And maids in the highrise hotels where the dragon reigns.
Such islands of death must be shunned. We must seek

The place of goats and sheep by the sea, narrow lanes,
No cars, hand-made-painted boats, fishermen on the beach
By the café where the iguana sips wine each day at noon.

Islands, as they distance themselves from blurred continents,
Promise sense of place and set-apartness. Sanctification.
Wholeness, where the sea's word is the sun's deed.
There are no therapists on the true islands, no need
For false priests and mobs of mystical masseurs.
No multitudinous mainland incarnations--sleazy healers,
Death-ofthesoul-Merchants in strip malls of self-actualization--
No interstate identity-mongers, TV and website prophets
Of Narcissism, no raving avatars of transmogrification.

Islands, as they sing their secret names across forgotten
Maps, are sufficient to the necessary rage for change.
Like Parris Island, where you changed overnight on a fifty-
Mile forced march in the cadence of the snakey swamps.
Like Koh Samet, in the Gulf of Siam, roadless wilderness, nothing
But the thatched hut where you sleep and the six-foot lizard
Comes from the jungle to tremble and shake your hut at dawn.
Like Ushant, ancient Celtic stone-circle, fogbound, where sudden
Sun dictates the Code of Manners that commands your island-rage.

Islands, as they burn in the bright noon of the flesh,
Draw down and drown the dark night of the soul.
Dive under the wave, ride spindrift surf to shore: this makes
Us new — Strict ritualists of tides where the hurricane heart
Knows the slow exactitude of sacraments of sun, sea, sand, salt,
The langorous litany of lassitude that must precede
Deep shapeshifting change. Seabirds fly, fish leap beyond the reef,
Ordered by island shapes, submerged borders. Owning such order,
Such bright particularity, such sea-change islandicity, we are reborn.

One Day at the Beach: Strathmere 1999
(for R.M.N.)

I
The strange arithmetic of chance
The curious calculus of place
The ancient algebra of wind and wave
The bonesetting reunifying dance:

>Counting culmination waves, diving
>Under, riding ashore, gathering shells,
>Broken, more whole in halves
>Glistening in the water
>Under the sun that is un-
>Concerned with shadows
>Al-jabr -- the ancient science
>Of bones and reunification

II
Wind and wave contend
With light that bends
Like time in the soul's millennium.

We live, if we live, a thousand years
In a single well-made day
Crafted by will, chance, pure epiphany.

But we must not tell the others this.
Old Rage forbids informing the New Age.
We must hold it secret like a first kiss.

Upwelling
(for G.B.N.)

For someone who has spent so much time at the beach,
It's odd how hard it is to say why, in late July,
The water turns suddenly cold in a heat wave,
And the fish die, and a riptide swallows a child
On a perfectly calm day. It has puzzled me

For years, these indwelling secrets of the sea.
Perhaps you have noticed it, too, tried to explain
To your children. Maybe you even know about
Phytoplankton, how when the upwelling occurs
It sinks to the bottom, uses up oxygen

As it decomposes, killing the layered fish.
I walked by the shore one day and met a young man
With a rocket on his shoulder, his eyes on fire
With science. It was not a rocket he explained,
But a REMUS (remote environmental

Measuring unit), a torpedo-shaped robot
Used for offshore research, an undersea window.
Cutting-edge technology to study what used
To be mystery: UPWELLING and its consequences —
The warm water pushed out to sea, the cold come up

From the ocean floor. I thought I understood at last.
It is never too late to learn how the sea turns.

December 999 A.D. -- Millennial Troubadour with Bag of Bede-Bones Sings His Song

Listen my friends! For a flask of mead I will tell how the world ends.
Gather round all folk of Engla-lond who long to go to Jerusalem
Or Rome for Doomsday, to sing the universal cry "Veni, Domine Jesu!"
As Satan breaks his thousand-year chains and the AntiChrist reigns.
Lo! Behold many wyrd-signs and omens, heed in breast-thoughts the portents.
In Aquitaine the sky has rained blood, crimson stains that cannot be washed
From garments. In Far France it has stormed stones in one place for months.
Earthquakes, meteors, eclipses, savage tempests, they say, bespeak God's wrath
And the world eftsoon will burn away to airy ashes. Already it is hotter
Here in Engla-lond (and everywhere) than ever, hot like the hell-fire South.
If we survive, they will plant vineyards in York and Orkney. And the far North
Country is melting — today Sailors seek New Lands through old unlocked ice-
Fields but they cannot flee beyond the Ken of Satan. I will sing now of signs
I have seen with my own eyes. I, Wulfgeat, earth-bairn of Bishop Aelfwold
And Aelfflaed, noblewoman who owns and works and oversees great estates.
They my blood-borne parents, give wealth away, free all slaves and, prostrate,
They pray night and day as the Hour of Judgment swift approaches: Y1K.
I have seen the world's largest slave-market in Dublin and there I have seen
Many slaves set free, bright rings discarded as men made ready on their knees.

Hwaet! I have witnessed with the Nuns of the North fierce fiery armies
Fighting in the sky; and the world-sky split by a fat lightning bolt
Then a dark dragon with blue feet roaring from the torn firmament.
Hwaet! I, poor troubadour and loyal unready subject of King Ethelred Unred
(Well-advised ill-advised), have seen that image of Christ weeping bloody
Tears and the Wolf that crawled to the altar in Adoration — and I watched
That beast bite the bellrope, ring the Church-bell all night, and I know men
Who heard and never slept again. Armageddon is at hand, Apocalypse is near.
Thus we must fight the fiends of Gog-earth where the devil dwells below
The girdle, women walk wantonly in short dresses, men move through degeneracy
To mewing effeminacy. Fraud, violence, corruption rule this mundus senescit,
This world ripe for oblivion. Before it is too late, heed the Songs of the Saints.
— "Haefst thu bones to sellenne?" — Ic haebbe here in this bag many mystery-bones
And magic bones of Venerable Bede given me by Tyneside monk. And locks of hair
From Mary of Egypt, sovereign cure for Lust. And Thorns of the Glastonbury Tree
That I have seen in blazing bloom at Midnight this past Christmas Eve.
All this I sing and offer, Against the End, for clothing, shelter, food, mead.

New Year's Day Y2K/Y1K: Transpositional Millennial Dawns and Doomsday Hangovers

I am alone on the beach by the sleepless sea hungover in the Sands of Time
At the dawn of New Year's Day 2000 in Bimini. I watch far away the last
Disappointed Atlantis-fans lingering near the mysterious still-submerged stones.
All night they drank and sang up the stones, chanted weird Doomsday hymns
To Atlantis-rising while we sang and read poems at the End of the World Bar.
The whole world has a millennial hangover, I think, and my head aches as I read
From an old manuscript by the Gulf Stream. It is said to be authentic, unearthed
Recently and translated, a First Millennium poem about a troubadour's bag of bones.

I sit there, reading it aloud: a man emerges from the surf, listens, asks me
"Where did you get my song?" "Oh is this yours? Where's your bag of phoney
Bede-bones?" We get on fine, discussing Millenniums, his, mine, and what he'd
Been doing since he wrote the poem I held in my hand. "Well, when New Year's Day
1000 dawned and all things remained the same folks were frustrated, confused.
But they had to go on. I entered a scriptorium, semi-monastic, transcribing holy
Words. At first I embraced the old proverb: 'Every sacred word written, the devil
Is bitten, and sins are forgiven.' When they caught me wasting parchment writing

Down my own poems they kicked me out of the scriptorium. Still, well-made words
And songs remained my expiation." "What did you do then?" I ask as he starts
To build a sand-castle. "I went On the Road again, singing, storytelling; then
I saw things changing. Small things at first. Like we all began to bathe five even
Six times a year. There was more food. They talked of a New World. Waves of hope
Washed over the earth, dreams of rebirth. I shipped out on a sea-voyage, a man
Named Leif was captain. Before he found the New Land I was washed overboard.
I thought I was dead. Next thing I knew this vast strange ship picked me up —

It was larger than a village, on fire with bright lights like none I'd seen
Before, bizarre people and music, enough food to feed the world a feast. A sign
Read: 'Millennium Cruise.' That was yesterday, I think, but I am confused about
Time, Eternity, and other unthinkable things. I jumped from that weird ship
Near a place named Miami; I couldn't take the noise as they all blew harsh horns,
Drank something called Champagne, danced and kissed lasciviously, sang, groaned
Offkey about some Auld Lang Syne. And now I am washed up here. Tell me, please,
Am I in Hell or Paradise?" "This island is called Bimini. And you have

Jumped a thousand years: This is Y2K." "Speak English, please." When he was cool

With everything, I asked him about New Year's Eve 999, where he was, what he did.
"I was in Rome, at the old basilica of Saint Peter for Midnight Mass. Had a good
Day working the street, singing, peddling relics. The Church was mobbed with
Trembling weeping worshipers fearing the Day of Wrath. Some dropped dead right
There on the Church floor. Others were in Ecstasy expecting to see Christ return
At any moment. The Holy Father, Pope Sylvester, was magnificent. (I knew him,
A hell of a good guy, when he was Gerbert of Aurillac. Met him on the road

In France. We swapped songs and stories.) Anyway, he was splendid and when he
Elevated the Host as the bells tolled Midnight — Nothing happened. The Church
Stood firm, no fire fell, the earth did not open and swallow us. We lived.
Friends and enemies exchanged the Kiss of Peace and then we drank and danced
All night in the streets as all the bells on the Seven Hills of Rome kept ringing.
Sweet relief. Bad hangovers." "Tell me truly," I said, "about your bag of bones."
"So maybe some were phoney but maybe some were real." He seems a little offended.
"Tell me what harm there is in buying and selling relics and belief? Those bones,

Those thorns, those saint-strands of hair I sold with my songs — what harm in such
Song, such prayer? Maybe I am immortal, if that's what my being here proves,
Because of song, Bede-bones, Sacred Thorns, Saintly locks of hair. We all made
Them holy together by believing more than we doubted. Check out your world --
Your tacky phoney TV saints and relics." We checked it out and we agreed. Then
We went to eat at the café by the sea. He was amazed at rare strange foods he'd
Never seen or heard of: spinach, broccoli, cauliflower, brussels sprouts, potatoes,
Tomatoes; coffee, tea, chocolate and sugar. I explained the Age of Crusades,

Pilgrimages, Voyages, Science that brought these things. Then told him about Leif
Eriksson and America, what he'd missed by going overboard before the Fortunate
Landfall. He watched short people passing by, said in his day all were tall
Like him, like me. We discussed human shrinkage, the Black Death, crowded cities,
The Industrial Age, overpopulation, pollution and genetic decline. I reassured
Him with evidence that people were growing tall again. He reminded me that Global
Warming was worse, or better, in his day. We discussed the facts of the "Little
Optimum," how the world grew very warm after the First Millennium, how that made

All things grow until the long cold decline began in 1300. He resumed his script-
Orium Troubadour mode: "In the short view the only thing that doesn't change is
Change. In the long view, good things remain the same, for if we wait, they come
To us again. Whatever else you do, whatever changes, ends, returns, you must keep
Singing. Language changes, and we change with it, but the deed of song does not
Change." Above the beach, echoing off the Gulf Stream, we hear Church bells ringing.

"Are there Wolves in Atlantis?" he asks. "Only one wolf and in that Church," I say, "Because you put him there." "This has been fun," he says, heading into the sea:

"Hangover cured. If Atlantis rises, or if it doesn't, let's do this again
In 3000, OK?" "Fine with me," I say. "See you in Y3K. Later Wulfgeator."
"We can do it, you know, if we keep on singing." I salute. He dives under.

Sea-signs and Sky-writing: Sundown, January 1, 2000

Late in the day, by the wrinkled Gulf Stream,
We gathered on the beach. Some were relieved.
The Bowl Games and Parades and New Year's day —
All almost over and we were still standing,
The sea still streaming, the sky still serene,
(Those who were not relieved were disappointed
Atlantis had not risen. But they'll endure,
Find other islands, other magic dates).

And then, in the soundless sky above the skirling sea,
Low on the sunset horizon, these words
Appeared: "Fooled You! Wait Until Next Year!"
Cloudy, smoky, ragged words, edged like old-time
Sky-writing, but there was no plane, no agent.
"Maybe it will be January 2001.
Maybe you'll try again to end it all in 2068.
Haven't you learned yet there is NO TIME?"

Words drawn up from the sea, and sinking down,
Back to the vast inkwell of spindrift showers.
The sky-writing faded with the sunset.
The sea screamed like some ancient bagpiper
Skirling the haunted modal amplitude of time.
Sharks slid and glided like iceskaters towards
The darkening beach as we climbed the dunes,
Questing the exactitude of Happy Hour.

"Census 2000: Notice of Visit"

(Form D-26 U.S. Government Printing Office)

The card is stuck in my frontporch screendoor:
"Census 2000 NOTICE OF VISIT
Dear Resident: SORRY I MISSED YOU." Big,
loud type. Census Bureau wants to count me,
but I wasn't home. I can provide required
information by phone, call the headcounter.
His name scrawled on the card, hours when I can
call him: 9 AM to 10 PM. Clearly,
he has no other job. The card also says:
"Your privacy is protected by law
(Title 13 of the United States Code)."
If I don't call, the card threatens,
the headhunter will stop by again.
I'm trying to finish a book of poems
And get the garden in, so I d not call.

Two days later, I'm weeding th garden,
planting tomatoes, toward undown,
racing against the darkness. Earth-intense,
I look up from a hill of Yukon Golds,
see him standing there, his census badge
dangling from a chain around his neck. Says:
"I'm so- nd-so with the Census Bureau
And I'm here to fill in this form." He taps
his clipboard. I stand up, check his badge, glance
at his form, say "Go a ad Make it quick.
I've got work to do before dark." I answer
the questions about the house, who lives there,
who owns it. I'm thinking as I study him
that I left all the doors open in the house:
my house is far away from my garden

so this dude had to walk around my porches,
all over my property, to find me.
Maybe he's been inside my house. I check his badge
again. "Now, Sir, I must ask you your GENDER.

I am not permitted to verify this visually."
I laugh: "You're kidding, right?" "No Sir, the Census
Bureau does not kid." "OK write down POET."
He studies his little form. "Sir, the government
does not recognize that GENDER." "You sure?"
He shows me the form. "OK, write down GARDENER"
"Sir, the Census Bureau does not enumerate that GENDER."
"Enumerate this. Write what you want. I don't like
the question. Tell your boss that gender comes
from beget, to make things grow; I'm engendering
my garden and you're in my way. There's work

To do before dark. Don't forget some languages
have twenty genders — gender, genre, go home
and check your dictionary." Irritated,
I kneel back down in the dirt, pull some weeds,
toss them in a pile at the garden's edge.
He moves closer, stands there, weeds landing
at his feet. "Sir, now I must ask you your RACE.
I am not permitted to verify this visually."
He reads the categories. I keep tossing weeds.
"That's a racist question," I say. "Don't you read
The New York Times?" "No, Sir." "OK write down
POET." "I do not find that category,"
he says, looking at his little clipboard.
"Write it in, then." "I am not permitted
to do that, Sir." "OK try GARDENER."

"Sir, that classification does not exist."
This census dude is dense, tense, a Mensa reject,
and he never cracks a smile, just steps closer,
deeper in my pile of weeds. I've finished
up to a row of French leeks. I point to my sign:
"Do you see this — Race Real d'Hiver?
Do you know French? It means Royal Tribe of Winter.
Race means group, kind, tribe. I am of the Tribe
of Poets, the Tribe of Gardeners."
He makes his little sir-speech again,
unsmiling, so I know it is senseless
to go on. I stand up. We wrap the Census.
I'm feeling a little sorry for the guy,

obviously unemployed, taking what work
he can get. As he thanks me and turns to go

up the hill I say "Look. It's not personal.
I'm sorry you have such a miserable
job." With all the wit and acuity
of a census-taking robot he replies:
"Have A Nice Day, Sir." I want to say look
pal, the day's over now, and you've ruined it.
But I say nothing. I watch him walk toward
my house, thinking I'm just the kind of guy
the Bureau warned him against, thinking also
they're paying this dude thirteen dollars
an hour to invade my privacy and property
— that's a lot more than the Marines paid me.
On recon, I tail him up the hill, watch
him back out my driveway, get his license plate,
check the house, secure terrain, lock the doors:

       then rush back down to the grinning garden.
       There's still some work to be done before dark.

II
". . .To Get Through It All"

Old Man at Bar Toasts the Millennium, Inscribes on Coaster,
Hands Me Haiku-list: "What is Necessary to Get Through It All"

Games   Friends   Cats   Songs   Dreams   Deeds
Love   Loyalty   (no betrayals)
Place-Rituals

three short poems

I

For An Aging Poet, Falling Dead on the Street, Too Soon at 60

(Tanka for David M. Stoneback)

Years before, he pub-
lished good poems. Now he tends
the Church Signboard. Posts:
"With Falling Leaves, All Nature
Grieves." The next week my father. . .

II

Endurance: Or, Daily Bread and Autumn Leaves

(Haiku for Sparrow)

She broadcasts the breadcrumbs:
Flocks of sparrows descend
like wind-driven leaves.

III

On Plums, Mice, Cats and Dr. Williams

(for my American Literature students)

A.
Do you know the taste of a ripe plum,
Just before the moment of rot,
The glazed wet plummy color,
The tenacity with which the last bit
Of Impressionist Plumflesh clings
To the seed, resisting voracious
Toothsome efforts to suck it to the stone?
Committed to earthiness, *rien que la terre*,
Why do we not devour the stone?
For the same reason my cat, a fierce alert

And savage mouser, earthy and intellectual,
Always neatly and completely, sacra-
Mentally, devours the mouse, leaving
In strategic locations only that
Bloody plumstone head with two open eyes?

B.
This is just to say, Dr. Williams,
That your plums are no longer in the icebox.
We have taken down your grocery lists, Carlos,
Dumped all refrigerator-magnet verse.
It cannot be recycled. That landfill is closed.
Stick it in your red wheelbarrow, Doc,
Beside the dead anthologies.

Ghost Writers in the Sky: For Poets Born During the War

(and for David M. Stoneback)

Have you scanned all the thin poets in fat anthologies
Checking to see if writers your age
Or younger are included, thus measuring
Your literary fate against the academic page?
What is it about being born during the War?
I check all my anthologies. I find
Dozens of poets born in '38 and '39 —
Then a gap until '48 and '52,
Then swarms of poets born in and since the 60s.
So I ask what the hell's going on here?
Did God, or His Sister who edits
All the anthologies, decide no poets
Would be born during that terrible World War?

I remember Pearl Harbor, maybe, just barely.
In fact maybe I was there, five months old,
Swathed in swaddling Blackout Curtains,
Singing, trying to trade poems for guns.
That's the first thing I remember, those Blackout
Curtains, and peering furtively into blackness, waiting
For enemy planes to bomb and strafe our dark street.
Then I remember my father being arrested
For lighting a cigarette on the blacked-out boardwalk.
There were submarines out there, lurking just off shore.
Then I remember eating a line of invading red ants,
Marching on the windowsill, and teasing them,
And Marlene Dietrich amusing the troops.

I remember Mairzy Doats and Dozey Doats
And I remember Roosevelt's death.
All the bold headlines. And then how my father
Took me down in the basement near the cool
Coal-bin that August day, how he shuddered
As he showed me the headline and the great cloud
And said "Nothing will ever be the same again."
And showed me where Hiroshima was
In the big old Atlas he kept in the basement

Near his trunkloads of 78 records.
My father was a poet, musician,
So I knew very early in life
Why mushrooms were kept in dark cellars

And how they mysteriously exploded
And why Vaughan Moore and Frankie Laine sang
"Ghost Riders in the Sky." At first I thought
They said "Ghost Writers" so I held the song
As my secret sign of writerliness.
About that time I announced to my father
That I was going to be a writer —
Maybe it was first or second grade.
He smiled, we sang "Yipee-i-aaa, Yippee-i-oo-o
Ghost Writers in the Sky." Years passed. *I knew* why Frankie
Laine sang "Mule Train" Hank sang cheating hearts and Elvis
Stayed at Heartbreak Hotels. Later my first hit song
In New Orleans was called "Big Cloud Hiding the Sun."

(Coda — to be sung)

Yippee-i-aaa, Yippee-i-oo-o, Ghost Writers in the Sky —
The writers loped on by me, I heard one call to me
If you want-a save your soul from hell in dead anthologies
Then writer change your ways today or with us you will ride
A-trying to catch the Devil's Word across these endless skies
Yippee-i-aaa   Yippee-i-oo-o   Ghost Writers in the Sky —

Has Anybody Here Ever Had A Frosted Mug Of Good Cold Draft Beer On A Hot Summer Day?

Has anybody here
Ever had a frosted mug of good cold draft beer
On a hot summer day?

Good, then maybe you know
All there is to know about writing.
You don't need an MFA.

Get the coolness in,
The frost, the taste, smell, wetness, the way
The mug shapes your hand.

Get the place
Where you drink it into the poem
And how it feels to stand

At the dark bar inside
When it's deadly hot and bright outside, and how the cool
Beer feels clean as it goes

Down, like whitewater, and the way her eyes
Look at yours as you say: "This beer is Shakespeare,
Or Hemingway's prose."

The Dreams That Linger

The dreams that linger
Are not the dreams of danger,
The spectacular, mysterious images
Of terror, horror, or the romantic
Dreams of innocence, virginity or lingerie:

The dreams that linger
Are of the simplest thus the strangest things:
An unknown person handing you an apple
On an unknown village street;
Or of a colleague, whom you barely know,

And do not find attractive,
Combing your hair, combing it long
And longer; or of Joe DiMaggio,
His dream-face as vivid as your father's,
Saying "Kid, the way you stand there

Why even bother to swing the bat?"
Or of mowing the lawn with Floyd Patterson;
Or of an old man talking to you about moonrise
Over the lake at the cottage he calls Shangri-La
(In a funny dialect that sounds like "hungry-ah")

He stands by his lake cottage where he lived
Forty years with his wife who just died
And says all night long in your dream
"Sometimes that old Moon come roaring across that lake
Like a one-eyed Padoodle Truck bearing down on me."

Or the dream is of your old cat, who has slept
With you for 17 years, turning toward you, looking
Up from the Sunday Times Sports Page he is reading,
Saying "Listen to this, will you". He reads a passage.
You both laugh. You wonder why your cat has waited

> Seventeen years to talk.
> But you say nothing.
> In the dreams that linger
> You always say nothing.

The Shape of Dreams

Dreams, like certain days, have a shape
We all too rarely ascertain.
The dreams we remember best
Are shaped like islands:
Some are country islands, Huck Finn islands thickly
Forested; a savage ship, *bateau ivre*, in a vast river
Or lake — impenetrable conflicted wilderness.
Other island dreamshapes are jewels in a crystalline
Sea, all sand and surf and sun-simple song.
The best dreams have the shape of ancient
Urban islands, stonebuilt, deep form, great structure

Shaping the complaisant river that flows by.
Like Ile de La Cité, Ile Saint-Louis,
Lucid linked islands in the Seine-stream.
Narrow streets and massive trees, seats of power,
Homes, prisons, cafés, markets, dreamstone towers;
Many bridges, gossamer webs vibrating to mainland;
Many barges and boats — silently gliding under arches.
(In your dream you think there are thirty three
Arches; it is delight, epiphany; awake it is impossible
To confirm and you don't know why it matters.) What matters
Is the way you possess lights of passing boats, trembly

Riverine reflections on old facades, homes where Baudelaire
Did opium and quested *Otium* (*sans dignité*).
If the dream permits an aerial view
The island dreamscape is more discenible:
Triangulated cartography leads past Baudelaire
And all the others, leads to the Cathedral
Where (in dreamshapes) you are able
At last to be fully present in the Mass
Like a medieval peasant or pilgrim.
Then dance down narrow lanes to joyous cafés
Where the bill never comes, you never have to pay.

Shooting Hoops with Emily Dickinson: or, the True Story of the Invention of Basketball

I know you think that basketball
Was invented just down the road from here
In Springfield, Mass. — close, but no cigar.
It was just up the road from here,
When once, long ago and yesterday,
I played the first game of basketball
With Emily Dickinson, in her Amherst driveway.

At first, I felt something of a fool,
Guarding her one-on-one in her tippet made of tulle,
Her bonnet, her long white dress.
She shot very deliberately —
Bucket foul shots, two-hand set shots —
She played very New Englandly
Till she took off her tippet and bonnet.

Then I suggesed a game of D-U-C-K-S.
We exhausted the prosody of hook-shots,
Reverse lay-ups, fadeway jumpshots, inventing
Everything as we played. Then she suggested we play
H-O-R-S-E — I was a little nervous at the mention
Of horses, what with carriages passing in the street,
And the kids shouting in the schoolyard.

When I tripped on her long white dress
I went down hard: she tended my skinned knees,
Went in the house for peroxide and, she said,
"To slip into something — more comfortable —"
I will confess I had wondered how she played
In that dress, tight buttons down the back,
And the corseted complexity of her underclothes.

When she came back out, with a cold Budweiser,
She was dressed in frayed cutoff jeans, very short
Shorts with slits up the side and a discreet unpatched
Hole near the back pocket. Now she dribbled through her legs,
Behind her back, every move set off with dashes.
She hit me with perfect passes going to the rim —

We invented the Emily Oop, the slam Dickinson Dunk.

We played another round of one-on-one
And now she was a Route of Evanescence —
And as I watched her I felt a Blue
Uncertain stumbling Buzz — my jumpshot failed —
I turned all Zero at the Bone.
"I like your look of agony," she said, as she won
The game with a perfect oblique hook-shot.

Until the setting sun, we sang each other as if we
Were old hymns — and that is how basketball was invented
In that certain slant of light in Miss D's driveway.
Games over, the dashes all used up, we stared at the goal —
Old whalebone rim, bits of tippet and worn-out corsets
For the net. We agreed the game was a sweet success
Although the goal could use some improvement:
       Still, it rippled like the flag of the defeated enemy
       In that driveway that held but just Ourselves and Immortality.

Fast Break
(for D.N.S.)

Down the great winds at work over the roofs of the land
Down the singing maze of the horror of living
Down the wringing wrists of the honor of living
Down the winding abyss of rivers of weary poets

Weaving the unresolved gestures of unfinished bards
Braiding and turning into deeds their undared dreams
Riding and rolling with the glistening motion of swimmers
Seeking the summation wave and the rim of immobile sands

Beyond the fraudulent soul and the flatulent flesh
Beyond wind into stillness breathless in sweet spots of time
Beyond the ancient chalice-rim circle of thirst
Within the susurrant murmur of the spiral of being

And the savage scoreboard clock mocks
The jubilant daughters of earth
Dreaming a new race of heroes

(1981)

Front-Porch Observations: Early Morning through the Screen-Door

It's not so much the way the squirrels fuss
In the yard, or the way the robins mess
Up the mulch in the garden, or the groundhogs
Move among zucchini and hollyhocks,
Fat in their Eight AM visions of green.
All that's too familiar, and when the screen-
Door slams like a gun, everything flies, runs
Like childhood dreams, like girlfriends becoming nuns.

It's more the way the Blue Jay soars in
For a highspeed smooth landing, like the Concorde,
And at the exact moment of touchdown
The flat sharp whack of the spring-coiled screen-
Door sends the Blue Jay five feet high, straight up,
As if the lawn had exploded at his touch.
I remember somewhere, sometime, in some sport,
In some game, moving exactly like that.

In the Garden of Baseball: Or, Phillies and Fishing

> "I aint an athlete. I'm a baseball player."
> John Kruk to reporter

(for Richard Davison)

That summer was all Phillies and fishing
All Greene and trout streams
All Incaviglia and reeling in big ones
All Daulton and caught one
All Eisenreich and rainbow strike
All Kruk and luck.

Well, almost all:
There were precious trout
That got away
And Fregosi pouts
On certain days
With Mitch Williams ninth innings
Twilight relief when we slipped into sinning
With worms and wild pitches
Loading the bases and the cooler with dinner.

We fished always till near dark
So on the long drive down from the Catskills
We could get the Phillies
On the truck radio. After eight, they came clear.

We gathered rocks from every stream we fished
To build a waterfall in our yard.
During afternoon games, we stacked the stones
Shaped the pond and waterfall
While the Phillies played oldtime ball
Building a season like a fine drystone wall.

That summer was all fishing and Phillies
And sometime gardening:
All Hollins and onions
Morandini and zucchini
Mulholland and tulips
Williams and Impatiens

Amaro and Poireaux
All Kruk and Leeks
All Lenny Dude and Plenitude.

And among the streams and mountains
Among the leeks and corn
With powerful radio
Poised among hills of potatoes,
Terrifying strange beetles and bugs,
Edenic syzygy of earth and air
Appled Adams and Eve-grieving airwaves
Transcending space and pommes-de-terres
A rare second innocence,
A strange glory was reborn:
Listening to perhaps a hundred games
Through thunder-static and frequency-drift,
More games than I've heard since the Whiz
Kids ruled 1950, all down the long falling seasons —

That summer when the Phillies reinvented baseball
I learned again that baseball is a ritual
That dies on TV
That lives on Radio
That lives in the homerun voice of Harry Kalas
That lives in the homespun jokes and stoic
Calls of Richie Ashburn (who signs all autograph
Requests, as he did for me in 1950)
That lives like Big Boy and Jet Star tomatoes
That lives in stadiums like Victory Gardens
With scoreboards like waterfalls
And every out
Is a leaping trout
Every hit, every home run
Is the heartstopping Big One
In Oh! the whitewater freedom
Of fishing and gathering water-smoothed
Rocks rounded like baseballs in the Catskills
Harvesting vegetables like unbroken circles
Perfect and smooth as the ultimate O
In the sweet slow Garden Summer
Of Fishing and the Phillies.

Gardening is the Number One Sport
(for Bob Lewis)

Gardening is the Number One Sport, isn't it?
More people play it than any other game.
It has all the required signs, designs:
Tryouts, Spring Training — that's forcing things
Into the ground too early in the season.
Making the team is getting the soil right,
Knowing what to plant where and the right time.
Then the season really begins — everything grows
Till the Colorado Potato Beetles, the New York
Groundhogs or Boston Bambis sweep a series, knock
You out of first place. Weather is like a high-school
Cheerleader squad — sometimes rainy, sometimes sunny
Disposition, partly cloudy, isolated thunderstorms,
Extended drought. Highschool athletes spend too much
Time watching cheerleaders. Gardeners spend too much
Time watching the weather channel.

Maybe green onions are bunts,
Zucchini and red-leaf lettuce are infield singles,
Some tomatoes are ground-rule doubles,
And fine fat heirloom tomatoes are triples.
A strong stand of leeks, overwintered Poireaux
Explode in May like Home Runs. Around the All-Star
Break, there's the garlic crop, a grand slam,
Bases loaded with the first new red potatoes.
Of course, all fans, all gardeners keep score
In their own eccentric ways. You fill in the blanks
Your way: Beans or peas or rare flowers,
If that's your thing, can be your doubles or triples.
And every gardener strikes out, maybe on rare roses,
Or gets called out on strikes by Broccoli worms,
Gets skunked in dark earth-innings, loses a whole row
Of something or other in a Groundhog-to-Bambi double play.

One important thing, often overlooked, is the mulch,
How you fight the drought, contend with weeds — a lot
Like fans, or maybe sportswriters. I use newspaper
For mulch, it feeds the soil — only certain sections

Of some newspapers, the right paper and ink, no color.
The New York Times Sports Pages and Help Wanted work
Just fine: "All the News that's Fit to Eat."
There is a distinct satisfaction in knowing that all
Those statistics, boxscores, batting and earned run
Averages will rot into my dirt by the end of the season,
When I harvest the October potatoes: holding up fat
Peruvian Blues and Yukon Golds like World Series trophies.
After the long summer of penance in the dirt, I reckon
Harvest is like Victory. The sacrament of storing potatoes
In the wine cellar under braided garlic pennants
Helps get me through the endless winter to spring training.

From Petanque Poems

> (A sequence of petanque, or jeu du boules, poems
> dedicated to all boulistes in France & the world)

I

It's a fine French game of earth and air
Of steel balls (no bumbling Bocce-wood), very hard ones.
They play it lucidly, luminously, in the Luxembourg Gardens,
In every lambent village square.

II

For Lawrence Durrell, Having entered the Holy Silence of the Bouliste

Contemplating a lecture I had promised to give
At the Papal Palace in Avignon
About Lawrence Durrell and Boules
And other quintessentially French things,
I remembered the look on Larry's face
The last time we saw him at his place in Sommières.

In his kitchen, over the last liters of local wine,
We spoke of the Socratic austerity of the silence
Between the throws of the village boulistes.
He said that when he finished this last book,
He would retire, take up the game in earnest.
He would study the holy silence of the bouliste.

I did not have my petanque balls with me
So he made me promise that on the next visit
We would play an austere Socratic game in that sacred silence.
Two years later, after my boules-centric tribute
To Larry at the Papal Palace
It was my darkly decorous duty to read his final poems

For the crowd gathered
At his graveside ceremony.

I would have preferred to go alone,
To place one ball, one steel sphere,
On his unmarked grave
(A three-striper, for irony and good measure).

Just before facing the crowd, I went alone to his walled
Garden to keep my word.
I tossed a few balls, high arcs, slow rolls, backspins,
Hoping they all pleased him
In the steely serene interval,
In the holy silence of the bouliste.

III

Bimini Boules

(for Don)

The first day at Bimini
We walked the entire intimate island
Looking for the correct terrain.
We found it, a perfectly level hardsand terrace
Above the sea, overlooking the streaming Gulf,
With foliage discreetly arranged,
Sunsets not too insistent.
It happened to be in front of Thomas Hudson's
House, from Hemingway's *Islands in the Stream*.

On the last island, the week before,
There had been soured games
With old friends who had forgotten how to play
Who betrayed
All games, order, measure, form, and joy.
The silent watchers, the Club Med drifters,
The locals, the Governor's Harbour fishermen,
Studied the conflicted rhetoric of play, the singing steel,
As if bemused in some dream of Martin Eleuthera King.

In Bimini, we found the perfect player.
He made it seem unnecessary to pray

For an old friend who had lost all loyalties.
The new player shared our sense of form,
Ritual, communion, holy silences,
Poised competition, and precisely measured
Joy. The games, while they lasted,
Were so sufficient that we forgot the ghost
Of Hemingway, though he played with us.

Playing Boules by Quartz-light at 4 AM: (Or, Why We Play Games
When There Is Nothing You Can Say That Would Be True Or Even Useful
In A Brotherly Way)

(for D.K. & Schuyler)

It was hard to see le cochonnet,
The little pig, the petanque pill, playing uphill
Into the quartz spotlights at Four A.M.

We sat on the frontporch rockingchairs
For hours, talking, after a dinner
That was a kind of celebration,
Mixed, as most are, with uncertainties
And half-uttered undertones, unsayable
Things perhaps, about fatherhood, motherhood:
The importance of names on birth certificates;
About legally mandated child support,
Seventeen percent of the father's salary;
About who would and wouldn't marry and why;
About how to break the news, and who to tell.
That is, these things were in the air, but we,
The men, said very little about them.
Women, they say, know better how to talk about
Such things. After two bottles of Gigondas,
Supple, Rhône-born, of sun-drenched granite soil,
After a quart of Havana Club Rum,
In the rockingchair quietness of the porch,
It was very late and colder than hell
For mid-June and the women who know how,
So it is said, to talk about these things,
Had all gone to bed. It was time, then,
With the last of the rum, for a game.
Clamping the new quartz-lights on the high backs
Of the rockingchairs at the edge of the porch,
We arranged the zones of light on the Four A.M. lawn
With great deliberation. Selected our balls,
And played, with grave precision, at the edge
Of darkness. Our shadows, like great black bulls,
Obscured the court when we crossed the light.
The zones of play required that we throw
Into the light, blinded, or into our own

Massive shadows — until we found the oblique
Angle of approach to the taurobolium.

It was easier to see le cochonnet,
The little pig, the boules pill, squinting
Obliquely in the crystalline Five A.M. light.

Under the game's discipline, he never asked
What would you do? When we wish to avoid
Words that sound so handled, so banal,
So used, soiled, exchanged, we play a game.
When all words we might utter fit a cartoon
Balloon, we say nothing, and play the game.
I do not remember if I half-said
That biology, once the animal imperatives
Have been satisfied, is nothing.
Do not recall if I said between throws of the ball:
Biology is nothing — Love is everything.
(And did I say that for every biological
Child I had abandoned, I had raised and loved
Another? Did I say I sometimes hear the knock
At my door of a long-lost son or daughter,
Coming to claim some biological
Birthright, a name, some dream-wish or blessing
I cannot, might not, bestow? OK, maybe
Biology is something, but Love is everything.)
Perhaps, between the poised steely exactitude
Of throws, we may have joked about fatherhood
As we played along the sword-edged lines of darkness,
As we slapped mithraic mosquitoes seeking
Blood-knowledge, too, seeking the limits of necessity.
I remember thinking about a poem
I'd been working on that day, trying to get
The exact feelings and pressures of swimming underwater,
Then swimming, diving, trying to observe as I dived,
Learning that it was impossible to think
Underwater, about being underwater.
There was only the mystery: you had to surface,
And render it, understand it later.
Maybe that was like the fatherhood that had
My boules-brother so worried. Later, he would

Surface, when his son was born, and Love would
Be everything. But I did not say this,
We just played the game, ritual exultation in the kiss
Of steel on steel, steel on pill. Shall I say I let
Him win? No, he beat me for the first time. . .
Like once, years ago, when an old friend suffered
Tragedy, could not talk about it, only said
"Let's shoot hoops" and he beat me, one-on-one,
The first and only time. Or when another
Old friend, in a season of conflicted joy,
Could not talk, said "Let's go fishing" and he caught
The biggest glistening trout. That is the blessedness
Of sport, that is why we play games when there is
Nothing you can say that would be true
Or even useful in a brotherly way.

      It was easy, at last, to see le cochonnet,
      In bugblizzard, mothbombed light, luminous pill on the lawn,
      Playing into the wordless solidarity of dawn.

The Lost Regeneration? (Or, Getting Hip)
(for a Poetry Slam with the theme: "Regeneration"
& for Don Junkins)

"You are all a Lost Regeneration"
she said. The village explainer, she bored us.
She haunted us, the Vietnam Generation.

And now, old warrior-poets are getting hip
replacements, old jock-poets in surgery
dreaming of running again, dreams of glory.

I tell him, in his anesthetized hypnotic
state: "What with two new hips — hiphiphooray! —
you're a kind of Hippogriff and you must drink

from Hippocrene the sacred spring of poetry
and sing your surgeon's Hippocratic Oath."
He laughs. I wish him: "Happy Hip-Gnosis."

His mind wanders to his all-star football days,
to his endruns as Bobby Kennedy's
campaign manager. My mind meanders

thinking of physicists who say there is no Time.
Maybe we are Meanderthals from the late
Plasticene Age, chronosexual in our rage

against unbending bone, unfolding flesh,
chronophobic in our quantum gravity
yet there has been this to do, to make, to say:

"All well-made poems are Deeds of Regeneration."
And the old poet-hipster from Helicon
smiles: "We make our runs, slants, reverses, fast breaks,

we know that poems, unlike bones and joints,
cannot be surgically renewed with plastic —
but does this slam-poet generation

know or is it all hollow hyphopocrisy all money

and sex?" In great pain he shifts in his hospital bed.
He thinks of thirty years of teaching poets, poetry.

Eyes closed, in silence he listens to the rain, the storm.
I whisper "As long as words can form and hold
that sudden terror of winter thunder

and wonder, poets will perform their operations
with surgical precision, very hip —
don't worry about the kids, old friend

they know there's more to it than money drugs and sex
they know how the line rolls, how Time rocks the Heart and Soul
they know because we helped create Regeneration X."

Clearing the Fin-de-Siècle Death-Tree from the Boules Court
(for Ed & Ann Marie Meisel)

For years we played in the shadow
Of the great dead oak
That leaned, each year a deeper bow,
Leaning down toward the lawn
Where we play Petanque.

Grass grew high in the lanes of the lawn
Where the massive tree might fall.
We were always aware when we mowed,
And when we played, measuring each throw
For the reach of the Death-Tree.

I grew fond of the tree, its familiar ragged bends,
Like some blasted tree in a favorite painting.
Several winters, I studied the broken V's,
First one great limb, then another,
Crashing down with the ice and the snow.

I suppose I was superstitious, hoping the tree
Would fall on its own, bow down in final veneration
Of the earth in hurricane wind or blizzard blow,
Dignified salute to dark victory, Nature's triumph.
At last, I had to mow, the tree must go,

The court had to be cleared for a *Boules*
Tournament. I was glad the chainsaw
Wouldn't start. This tree deserved the ax,
Lightning strokes like prayer,
Ritual calculations of all

The Geometry of the Fall:
Face-cut, lean, angles, how to minimize
Impact on the two-hundred year old stonewall;
How to read the measured curtain call, the last
Play of the fin de siècle Death-Tree as we struck

Toward the heart of its braided inwardness,
Bringing steely light to its tight-twisted core,

Cylinder of secret energy for a hundred years or more.
At least we did it like Primal Man, in the sweat
Of the crosscut saw, the ring of the ax, so we could hear

Its final speech, like some classic actor from the 1890s,
Coming apart slow and steady, whispering its last words,
Ripping, slowsplitting, coming untwisted
For three full moaning minutes before the ultimate
Crashing bow all the way down to the earth.

We worked so hard with wedges and dulled axes,
For four hours, that we had trouble breathing
In the terrific heat of the tree's fall.
Now, the tree-trace serves as referee, we *boule*
The brown lawn-line where it fell, acknowledge

Its sway and reach, there by the stone foundation
Trace, palimpsest, remains of the gazebo
From the last century. Unwilling to let it go,
To merely dump it down the hill, or burn it,
We chiselled some kind of garden sculpture,

Used other parts to make new raised beds
And planted late *pommes de terre*, apples of the earth.
One gigantic piece of trunk still waits
In the bushes to achieve its final form
Or burn in slow decay through the next century.

On Paintings and Cats

When I retired from poetry readings
In the Sixties, too many poets were doing
Poems About Cats, Poems About Painting.
I would rather pet, play with, or just observe a cat.
And I preferred to get my paintings in galleries, museums,
Not words. So I retired from reading, became a folksinger
And sang songs about dogs. Sometimes, of course, I took
My dog on stage with me, so deprived audiences
Could hear a real dog howl.

When I returned to the poetry scene a few years ago
More poets than ever were doing cats and paintings.
It was a rare peaceful night when some poet did not meow
About paintings, cats, every five minutes. It got so bad
You had to go to the Pound after every reading, adopt ten cats.
Then get out the brushes, paint all day in wordless rapture.
Last year, when I went on a book-promotion tour,
Agents and publishers, Reading MC's and audiences
Asked for poems about cats, poems about paintings.

It didn't matter that my poems were about springs
And cats don't like water. Why not make a poem,
Somebody said, about saving your cat from drowning
In a spring? Yeah right, I said, that and the Pre-Raphaelite
Painting I made of it. That was it. I knew I'd been wrong.
Clearly, since I cannot bring my cats, who are all famous painters —
Perhaps you know their Blue Period? — but they don't travel well
Like certain ineffable wines I prefer to drink at home,
I must sing a song of painting, chant the canticle of cats.

Le Chat Impressioniste

(With thanks to J.A.S., Supermarket Research Assistant)

I have a Chat Impressioniste
So French when he eats Fancy Feast
So idée fixe about Meow Mix
So civilized he likes French flicks;
So totally Toulouse-Lautrec
When at the café he reflects
On food and girls, on all things phoney,
Like dogs and disciples of Monet.

He detests Whiskas and Alley Cat —
Makes him see dots, Seurat and Signac.
He dozes through Kit 'N Kaboodle
Like a fat peasant in Breughel.
He rates Friskies with Velásquez
And Puss 'n Boots with Marcel Proust.
He'll tolerate Alpo, like Pablo
Picasso and sometimes El Greco.
He likes 9 Lives and Poussin-Boots.
And when he's in the mood for Titian
He'll sometimes eat Kozy Kitten.

Above all, an impressionist cat,
He likes his brush-strokes clean, his light fat.
He can move fast, he can move slow
Like stars, like suns in old Van Gogh.
He cleans his ears while playing cards
Disdains the cats that prowl the yard.
He studies form like Paul Cézanne —
Who knows what shape, design, weighs on
His mind as he eats Purina:
Renoir's girls at the piano?
The Louvre? or dancing the cha-cha
With some ballerina from Degas?
Or purring "Begin the Beguine"
To a Tahitian from Gauguin?

If Cats Could Talk

One of the other things about cats
Is their sense of discretion and privacy,
Like Joe DiMaggio, their extreme under-
Statement like Hemingway, their uncanny
Ability to express form and meaning
As they rest in silence. Unlike dogs and humans,
They don't bark too much. My oldest cat (he's 16)
Has such contempt for speech, for using the same wornout
Words, that he rarely makes a sound. If he wants
My attention, he opens his mouth soundlessly.
I return the gesture. We've had some great
Conversations like that. Like some humans,
Cats know how to enter a room in silence,
Almost always looking great, know how to walk
Across a room in that certain way.
In short, they have charisma, poise,
They know how to purr away all noise.

Or is it all just an illusion,
Would they really be like humans
If they started to talk? You know that cat
That sits serenely on the windowsill
Watching birds and squirrels all afternoon?
That would be Mr. Envirocat, giving Nature-Talks
To schoolkids. And you know that cat that sleeps
All day on the Norton Anthology — he may be a literary
Critic, giving endless explications de texte,
Writing in fat letters on the blackboard
"A Poem should not mean, but purr."
And then the Cat Poetry Readings
With cat-poets saying things like "Now I will
Read one of my obligatory human-poems. I just love
My human, I can watch him for hours, sometimes I wish
He could talk, but on the whole it's probably better
That he can't." The next cat would read poems about paintings.

Even worse would be the fat-cat lawyers on TV,
The representatives for the ACLU (the American Cat

Liberties Union), the separation of Church-and-State
Cats protesting the production of cat chow in the shape
Of little crosses, the PC cats lifting their eyebrows
At the unradicalized cats who insist on saying things
Like Persian Cat instead of Iranian-American, Siamese
Cat instead of Asian-American, Alley Cat instead
Of Homeless American, crook-tailed cat when they should
Say Tail-Challenged Cat. Then, of course, the cat-athletes
In post-game shows answering questions about their leaping
Ability, talking about themselves in the third person
And thanking Mama. And the Country Music Cats accepting
Their Grammy Awards and thanking God. Cat-actors
And producers and directors, wallowing in clichés,
Filthy rich, wondering if they can score as many bucks
From their new musical "Dogs" as they have from the endless run
Of "Humans." Of course, there would be cats doing cute human
Commercials, cats on Letterman doing stupid human tricks,
Cats showing goofy humans on America's funniest
Home videos. And the endless talk shows, "meow, meow"
(I hurt, I hurt) talking about kitten abuse and tomcat
Date rape and all the rest. There might be a hair
More dignity to the cats in tight black collars
Discussing catechism and moral cataclysm, arguing
The finer points of gendered address in prayers
And hymns — you know, the great "Our Feline Father"
Debate, should it be "Our Cat Who Art in Heaven"
Or "Great Lion"? And they all join paws at the end
And sing "Amazing Cats." Then there would be the cat-
Soldier, interviewed from the front lines, saying "I regret
That I have but nine lives to give for my country."
Then the Gay Activist cats discussing catamites,
Whitewater fanatic cats on cataracts, religious cats on catacombs.

> Yet, as in all worlds, the worst by far
> Would be the cat-politicians. That charismatic
> Cat who sits on the wall and says things like

"Ich bin ein Berliner." That five o'clock shadow
Cat who growls things like "Peace with Honor."
Great Communicator cats who doze and purr
Through cabinet meetings. Wooden Indian cats

Born in Washington hotels who have never said or done
Anything that anybody can remember. Adviser cats
With slogans like "It's the Kitty Litter, Stupid."
Smiling, smirking, paw-pressing cats who work the crowd
On core domestic issues while the world goes to hell,
Who say things at phoney town meetings like "I feel your pain."
Who look in the camera and lie, and almost believe
Their own lies since they believe in nothing but themselves
Anyway. Who tell you endlessly "It's time to get back to
The work of the American Cats" and "I did not have
Sexual Relations with that Alley Cat."

Quick, somebody call the Animal Control Warden,
The Society for the Prevention of Cruelty to Humans.

What You Name Your Cats and How You Hold Them

Is there anyone here who loves cats? OK.
Is there anyone here who hates Hemingway?
Yes, I see. That's probably because you never
Read his work. But we'll get to all that later.

First, let me note that Hemingway loved cats.
Sometimes he had more than fifty, feeding
Them by hand from his dining-room table,
Giving them vitamins, writing poems

For them as they rubbed against his typewriter.
I see this has already changed your mind.
How can you not love a writer who loves cats?
(Did I mention that I love all my cats, each

One quite distinctly.) Hemingway's favorite
He named Crazy Christian, began a poem for him:
"There was a cat named Crazy Christian
Who never lived long enough to screw. . ."

But he knew all the secrets of life so
Of course "the bad cats killed him in the fall."
Study the famous photo of Hemingway
Holding Crazy Christian, his hand, his eyes

And you know more about the man than most
Biographers. Never trust a writer,
A neighbor, especially a biographer
Who does not know and love and hold his cat.

What you name your cats and how you hold them
Tells everything we need to know about you.
Your hands, your eyes, your vision, your power to name,
The infinite tenderness of your soul.

Les Baux Diddley

As cats will, he appeared one day at our backporch
Door. Ugly, scraggly, battlescarred face peering
In the screen-door. We fed him. He did not tell
Us his name. Since it is written that all cats
Must have names, we waited for his to be revealed.

He moves like cats are not supposed to move, awkward,
Graceless, like a three-legged dog. His head
Is too big for his body, but his face has a strange beauty,
Like a contemplative poet. At last, we knew his name
Was Les Baux, for he looks like the cats that stalk

The medieval ruins of Les Baux in Provence, near
One of our old homes, where cats stare from ancient stones,
Scraggy strays from the Courts of Love: postmodern bards,
Tail-end of a long illustrious line of Troubadour Cats.
His name, then, is Les Baux, though he seems to have

No voice, never makes a sound. And since he looks
Like the kind of cat who would play a red electric
Guitar with a weird shape, the kind of cat who knows
Only two guitar chords, one progression, E and D,
We finally understood his full name was Les Baux Diddley.

He waits every morning on the back-porch steps
And growls and hisses every time we feed him.
We have never touched him. But it is not just food he begs,
Since he sits there for hours, listening to our voices
In the kitchen, listening to the music on the radio.

Sometimes he sits on one step, his paws perched
On the next higher step, looking like an old monk
In solitary devotion. Even then he hisses, untouchable.
After all there are many kinds of cat, many ways to name
Them, many ways to hold them, many forms of love.

Azalea Alley, After the Tornado

(for Robin Gajdusek)

We cannot walk through our azalea alley
without snowing flowers all down around
our shoulders, gentle thornless May-bright burs
tickling eyes and hair, after the rare tornado
bent the tunneled blazoned branches so low

After five days of rain the wet sidewalk
is plastered with petals, glossy with blossom
Coming from the car with bags of groceries
you stop, say: "Look! it's like a Monet-pond.
Remember the water at Giverny?"

And it is, even if azaleas
are not waterlilies, the bloom-stunned sidewalk
is not a pond, New York is not France,
tornados don't have a chance in Giverny
or Normandy or wherever Monet really lived

Watching the Way Things Grow
(for Kaimei)

and die
watching the way things bloom
and fade

how leeks
explode from winter mulch, grow tall and fat,
go to seed

remembering April
how you sniffed the tight folds of lilac buds
seeking scent

and how
you got so bloody busy when they bloomed
and went

in a day
or three you barely had time to catch and hold
the aroma

and why
it is necessary to watch the way
things grow

"*Mort pour la Patrie*: Or, Looking for the War Memorial in New Paltz — Armistice Day 1998"

(for my Parris Island Platoon-mates)

It is Armistice Day (#80) and I drive
Around New Paltz in my pickup truck
On the Great War and Modern Memory Pilgrimage —
A Pilgrim in New Paltz, looking for the War Memorial.
No one can tell me where it is, where any of them are:
"What War? What Memorial? What Arm-stuss?"

This morning I happened to look at a photo
Of my favorite village in France,
Centered on the Memorial, the sign: *Mort Pour la Patrie*,
With the list of 45 men killed in the Great War —
Forty-five from this tiny village — *now* — of 17 persons.
Is it that sign, always remembered, always beflowered,

That gives that village its elegaic tranquillity,
Its centered sense of absolute peace?
And is it the disordered dead, the dishonored memory,
The discordant traffic of the eternal present,
History denied, forgotten, that makes this place what it is?
As I dodge traffic, looking for a sign, any sign

Of memory, I turn up the tapedeck volume
To drown out the honking horns and passing curses
As I pull over here and there to ask strangers
Where the War Memorials are. Then I sing along with Piaf.
I brood this century's one long war, the resonant artillery of history,
The lingering mustardgas of solipsism, trench warfare of acedia and anomie.

I think of today's news from France,
The political skirmishes of Chirac and Jospin,
The honor-glory debate — should the mutineers of eighty years
Ago be pardoned now? I think of Faulkner's *Fable*.
I feel my ill-fitting Marine dress uniform, holding me tight,
As I turned in my closely-argued 40-page Pacifism letter

And I see the twitch in the general's cheek

As he read my formal statement of conscientious objection.
I think of my friends in commando-training,
After I dropped my case, and try to count
How many went to Viet Nam, and how they came home.
I do not know all the facts, but most of them were lost.

I remember when my Marine Reserve unit
Was activated during the Cuban Missile Crisis:
Combat-alert, we bivouacked on the Gulf of Mexico,
Believing we would hit the Cuban beaches
At any moment. I remember how it felt
To get that hardship discharge the day we first bombed

North Vietnam. . .
And after that very morning no more Marine reserves
In my classification were discharged.
So, while I sang on Bourbon Street, wrote, built a log-cabin
In the wilderness, went back to college, my platoon-buddies
From Camp Lejeune and Parris Island went to Viet Nam

And most of them came home to have their names inscribed
On a Memorial somewhere down South, somewhere out West.
Suddenly, I hear our tightly-harmonized cadence,
And it calls up unknown ancestors dead in France,
Still bleeding into the soil, *mort pour la patrie*,
In the one long great war for "democracy."

Still searching for Memorials, I sing cadence
And the entire village, laconic streets, taciturn stonewalls,
The stoic traffic, the shops, malls and college halls
Echo, reverberate, out-of-sync-and-step, shout back at me
As I sing along with Piaf:
"Non, je ne regrette rien" (et rien et nada y nada)

What War? What Memorial? Everything says
And sings "C'est payé, balayé, oublié. . ."
Swept away, forgotten, but no, not paid for,
Not by us, not in our surreal denial
Of memory. It's not about glory. Just the simple choral
Cadence of remembering, finding, saluting the War Memorial.

Hunting on the Slopes of Kilimanjaro in Late Fall
(for Billy Collins, fishing on the Susquehanna)

That title may mislead you, I know,
But that's one thing poetry is supposed to do,
To help you find the way: I have never hunted
On the slopes of Kilimanjaro, not in late Fall
Or any season, or on any mountain-slope I can recall:

Though I have hunted woodchucks and snakes (and long
Ago deer and rabbit), I was a Marine Sharpshooter,
And yesterday I shot three groundhogs
On the downslope from my garden
Where they had destroyed the zucchini and hollyhocks.

All this is not entirely unlike
Hunting leopard on the slopes of Kilimanjaro.
And why go there, when here is so much closer.
Besides, in the spaces between what you read
And what you know, you can make it up in what you write.

Generally, most days, it's much better after
The hard twilight hunting
To go into your own house where you don't have to listen
To the leopard's odd and tiresome insistence
That you follow him to the House of God.

Dying Eagles Go Uphill

"An eagle goes uphill and when I ran this one down. . .
and held him with his eyes full of hatred and defiance I
had never seen any animal or bird look at me as the eagle
looked."   Ernest Hemingway *True At First Light*

All birds and beasts, the hunters say,
Run downhill when they are wounded and dying.
The groundhog I have just shot in my garden
Runs straight at me, downhill, though there are
Many other ways to run. Most people, too,
Run, or slide, downhill all their dying lives.
The eagle's the exception to the rule:
When he is hit and dying, unable to fly,
The hunters say, the eagle runs uphill
And when you approach he will try to kill
You with those talons to his last breath,
And fix you with the fierce defiant eye of hatred
(Or is it terror? Or a ferocious holding on to life?)
Or just the Naked Eye of Nature —
The force that drives the dying eagle uphill.

The Great Abrivado: Les Saintes-Maries-de-la-Mer
11th November 1997

(for Antje, Philippe, & Roger)

It was the largest abrivado
In history, they say, eleven
Hundred horses and eleven bulls
On the beach on the eleventh
Of November. We were in the saddle

For five hours, riding in from Cacharel
Through the Marais, then miles along the beach
To the Plage-Est. My horse was Mirage,
And he liked the sea. We splashed in the waves.
My first time on horseback in thirty-five years.

Wordless, timeless, that feeling in the wind:
Eleven black bulls, eleven hundred white horses
And the sea — we rode with the eleventh taureau
And Mirage took me in close, very close
To the horns — or did I take him in?

Woodsmoke in Aigues-Mortes: Late November
(for Catha Aldington)

We like the way the woodsmoke lingers
In late November in Aigues-Mortes
As the village draws in on itself,
Folds inward for winter: tourists gone, fires stoked.
Behind the medieval walls, smoke lingers, stays.
In Les Saintes-Maries, wall-less by the sea,
The smoke of kitchenfires and *cheminées*
Is more diffused, is blown quickly away
Toward Africa, out there across the Mediterranean.

We drive over to Aigues-Mortes once
Or twice a week for the best tobacco,
For wine and cheese, for the *Herald Tribune*,
For fine filets of Loup de Mer. Sometimes
We stop in Notre-Dame-des-Sablons,
Wet our fingertips in the font, salute
Saint-Louis, all golden in his chapel,
His candles singing in the dark, there in the church
From which he embarked on Crusades, aboard *Montjoie*,

His warship echoing the old French war-cry.
It is still my town, his statue whispers
On the quiet *Place*, as we cross the square
To the *Tabac*. I buy the last pack
Of my favorite pipe-tobacco, the kind
With the earthy toasted aroma that lingers. My friend
Tells me he will order more, maybe next week
It will be in. We drive out the south gate,
Watch the last golden light on the ramparts,

Above the saltbright-marshes of the Salins du Midi.
We circle the walls, consider every tower
In its particularity — the Tour de Constance
With its message: *Resister*. The Tour
Des Bourguignons, where they stacked the corpses,
And salted them well, to keep the rot and smell
Down. After we stop at INTERMARCHE,

She reads the headlines threatening war from Baghdad.
Driving toward Les Saintes, crossing at Sylveréal:

The full moon summons le Petit Rhône
To glory, to bedazzling joy. This moonlight
Makes it easy to see the white horses
In the passing pastures. The black bulls
Are hard to see. We are almost home.
Li Santi glows across the Marais.
Smoke from the last burning field of Fall drifts:
We like the way the smoke lingers, from afar,
In late November in the dark Camargue.

The Mistral and Memory at Les Saintes-Maries-de-la-Mer
(for Eric Forbeaux)

It is the wind, not just any wind,
Only the Mistral that blows away memory
Blows it far out on the vast estranging sea.
It is the wind, not just any wind

That seems to destroy short-term memory
Here in the Camargue, in Les Saintes-Maries,
Where we note this in the discourse of friends.
After two months of intermittent wind

We feel it begin inside, this daily loss
Of memory which is, perhaps, not a bad thing.
Not like forgetting the words when you sing.
More like approaching a familiar cross-

Roads, and suddenly forgetting which way
To turn. At first we thought it was the vin de pays,
The Vin des Sables du Golfe du Lion
(Lions playing on the far beaches of memory)

But now we know it is more fundamental,
It is the wind, the daily, weekly wind
Roaring down the Rhône with the weight of all
Europe, it is the Mistral. Then this begins:

As short-term memory recedes, true memory arrives,
Coming in from the sea with Les Saintes Maries —
Mary Salomé, Mary Jacobé,
Mary Magdalene, utterly alive,

Landing here in this bright white wall of wind
Near two thousand years ago: this vision
Lives in the eyes of gardians and gypsies
Who still see the Holy Marys and Sarah landing

Here in the wind, not just any wind,
Only the Mistral that blows away brief memory
That clears the mind for the winds of history
Here in the wind, not just any wind.

"NYPD Blue at Notre Dame"
(for Dennis Franz)

Christmas Eve, Midnight Mass at Notre Dame.
Huge crowds gathered for hours, waiting for Mass.
Behind me, I sense a familiar presence.
In my peripheral vision, I see
His folded arms, the way he shifts his eyes.
I know this man, but I cannot place him.
My wife whispers in my ear: "It's Dennis Franz,
You know, NYPD Blue?" I don't watch much TV.
No one else at Notre Dame recognizes him.

You will read in TV Guide that he is the best
Actor on television. You will read
About his "emotional depth." You will even
Read high praise for a season-finale
Episode in which he kneels and prays.
But you will not read in TV Guide
How one Christmas Eve in Paris he sang
The Mass, composed, deep inside the ritual.
He seemed pleased that no one knew who he was.

And then this happened. In the great crowd
A mother sat down on the floor with her baby.
We feared she might be trampled by the pressing
Swaying mob. Yet, somehow, as if Sipowicz
And NYPD Blue were working crowd control,
A space cleared, a radiant magic circle,
And mother and babe slept at the center,
Stretched out on the stone. Strangers took off coats,
Spread blankets. As we moved through the long Mass

Everyone in the Circle of Epiphany
Was touched: there were tears, smiles, radiant beams,
And even, as the old song says, glory streams.
And in the crowd, no one smiled more serenely
Than Sipowicz — no this was Dennis Franz.
Even if I don't watch much TV, I know
Who he is, who we all were, in that circle:
Christmas Eve, Midnight Mass at Notre Dame.
Oh morning stars together, wet dark streets shining.

For Henry de Montherlant in the Hospital, After a Cornada in the Bullring

It is December 1925 and I am sitting
In a Parisian cabaret, listening
To a singer, the *chansonnier* Bonnaud,
Sing his list of New Year wishes
For 1926: "let us hope. . .that
That bore Montherlant will publish only one
Volume and let us hope it will be posthumous."
You are in the hospital, Montherlant, spitting blood
After your *cornada*, your horn-wound in the chest,
Close to your lungs. You have been *aficionado*
Since you were thirteen, when you discovered
Tauromachia in Bayonne; you have performed
Well in the Plaza de Toros since sixteen
When the bullfight papers noted your work
In the *becerrada* at Burgos. At the next table,
They are talking about you, how your work is driven
By action, energy, discipline,
Rooted in the bullfight and the battlefield,
In Catholicism and Paganism, in the masculine
Brotherhood of war and sport.
When the singer repeats his line: "*Espérons. . .*"
— Montherlant will publish one posthumous volume —
The crowd at the next table, mostly young Americans,
Hisses the *chansonnier*, and one man glares
With hatred, stands up and shadowboxes
As if to destroy the singer and the taboo song.

Some months later, I am sitting in a café
On the left bank, reading *Les Bestiaires*.
Which is the talk of Paris. It is already
Being translated into many languages; in English
It will be *The Bullfighters*. I read the review,
Praising the "spiritual intensity" of your work,
Montherlant, speaking of the sacramental sense of passion,
The "profound religious ecstasy" in your novel,
The way you capture better than anyone ever
Has the ancient ritual of *toreo*. A mutual

Acquaintance has just left the empty café.
He brought news of you, said you were in hospital
Again, still suffering from aftereffects of the *cornada,*
And recurrent problems from your terrible war-wound,
The shrapnel still in your back from that artillery burst.
He said you were in fine spirits, pleased with the reception
of *Les Bestiaires,* the very picture of "repose in action."
Said you laughed as you proclaimed from your bed:
"We have had enough of flowery language and phoneyness."
Two days later he wrote all this in the newspaper.
He added something about your cult of authenticity,
Your vigorous and masculine prose,
Your spiritual stillness and poise under extreme pressure.
He added that, from your hospital bed, you declared
Your desire to found an Order based on Action *and* Meditation,
Passion *and* Gentillesse, Charity and Brotherhood.

So I am sitting here, Montherlant,
In the early spring of 1926, reading *Les Bestiaires,*
Pausing from time to time to let the French
Bloom and explode in my mind's ear as I look
Away across the river at the towers of Notre Dame,
Thinking, yes, this offers a way to live, a way to write,
Beyond all the phoneyness. I remember that *chansonnier,*
Curse him, and bless you, for writing, for living.
Before leaving, I stand at the bar to get some cigarettes.
A young man who has been watching me read your book
Comes up next to me, silent, shy, intense,
Not very tall, but very much there. He tells me his name,
Formally introducing himself in midwestern French.
I respond in English, for his sake. He says nothing.
Puts his big hand on your book, *Les Bestiaires,*
Taps it three times, says: "It's all in there."
No one knows it yet, perhaps no one will ever know,
But he will follow you and your Order all his days.
By the end of the year, he publishes a book
Called *The Sun Also Rises.*

For Max Jacob in the Concentration Camp at Drancy

Thinking of you, Max Jacob, trying to see
You at the *Lapin Agile* in Montmartre,
With Picasso and Apollinaire, trying
To make a new poetry beyond Symbolism,
With that avant-garde quaintness of Cubism
(Now, in fin-de-siècle retrospect,
It looks a bit that way) — but I am trying
To see you, Max, your visions, conversions,
While I sit in a New York hotel
At an academic convention
Listening to some third-rate intellectual
Dismiss your conversion as aesthetic
Religiosity. The professor drones,
Presumes, pronounces his sentence on two
Generations of poets, Catholic converts —
He lists and lumps them all together:
"Paul Claudel, T.S. Eliot, Charles Péguy,
Max Jacob, Allen Tate, Ernest Hemingway" —
"All these ecstasies," he spits, "mere aesthetics."
He speaks in the voice of a rejected
Gleeclub boy, has the face of an unsuccessful
Rapist, the mind of an unemployed engineer.

Tuning him out, I think of your humor,
Max Jacob, your skepticism, mysticism,
Your Faith, Love, Art, your will to "Perform
Miracles" with words, to "create a Celestial
Climate on earth." I hear your voice asking
Where are the old songs that teach us to hold love?
I hear your drunken Breton sailor, his *vantardise*,
Bragging, becoming Moses, Solomon, Christ,
Chanting invitations to Paradise.
I follow you to your monastery,
Max; you ask me if I know Meister Eckhart
And Saint Joseph of Copertino, flying
Like an airship, an ecstatic Zeppelin —
(The "Flying Friar," 70 witnessed levitations) —
And then you cry out "Je suis perdu!

Je veux aller à pied à Rome!" and Saint Paul
Makes the Pilgrimage with you, telling you
You are a God. Lost, alone in the forest,
You assign wild animals their parts, conduct
A concert which no one else hears. You bless
The choir, confirm the earth's celestial song.
Your song moves with the grace of a great river

      In the night — and here, in New York
      This third-rate academic drones,
      Unable to flow or fly with you,
      To Montmartre, or Saint-Benoit, or Drancy.
      I try to go with you to Drancy, Max,
      While the MLA executioner concludes
      And all I can do is bless you and try
      A prayer for you: Martyr, Saint, Poet, Man-God.

Vessels, Clamshells, Moonsnails
(for Linda Miller)

We walk along the beach observing the shells
That rattle and roll like shipwrecked vessels
Riding the back-and-forth motion of the surf.
She picks up a large clamshell: "This one's perfect
For an ashtray." I point to the neat round hole
In the shell. She discards it: "Damned Seagulls!"

I reckon I thought that once, long ago,
Before I saw the gulls conduct precision
Air campaigns: NATO-gulls strafing, bombing
The beach with clams. Hovering like Apache
Helicopters, selecting the exact patch
Of hard sand, the perfect angled moment

Of flight and height to drop and whack the clam,
To crack the shell in screaming ecstasy.
Halved, open, more lovely in their openness,
The wet shells shine in the spindrift sun.
I hold a shell in my hand, rub my thumb
On the neat round hole, explain the moonsnail's

Work — the grayish-white predator that plows
Through the sand in search of clams and mussels.
Sometimes five inches tall and blobby-long,
It has a massive retractable foot
That inflates with seawater, surrounds
Its prey with slimy foot, rides its clam-vessel

Through the night. Secretes acid to soften
The shell, then drills a hole with its radula,
Its raspy, toothy, tonguelike mouth organ.
What rough music of the moonsnail harmonicas
As they devour flesh through the apertures,
Then abandon ship, retract, slide inward

Behind resinous trap-door operculas.
Perhaps all knowledge is finally useless.
But exactitude is necessary.

Gulls scream at us, as if we are trespassers.
Flotsam and jetsam from some broken boat
Rides a loud wave washing over our bare feet.

Were they fishing when their boat was smashed?
Baiting hooks? Making love? Drinking? Praying?
On the TV, there are hurricane warnings.
Far out at sea, strange mountain-ranges rise.
An empty wine-bottle, firmly corked, rolls
In on a wave: voided Vessel of Mercy.

I hold it toward the sun, no message inside,
Nothing. (Maybe San Juan de la Cruz set
It afloat. Or Rimbaud in his Drunken Boat.)
Funny, how people used to be called vessels
Of this or that. I think of the old preacher
Who used to chant almost every Sunday:

"Lord we are poor storm-tossed Vessels of Imperfect
Knowledge: Teach us to be Vessels of Love."
We walk along the beach collecting the shells.
I have lost count but it seems that every fifth
Shell bears the sigil of the moonsnail.
Perhaps exactitude is useless

And only love is necessary.
We cross the dunes to the house. Wash the shells.
Later, the gulls are silent at last
As the orange moon rises over the sea
And vast tangerinetrembling waves crash and roar —
Hey Mr. Tangerine Moon play a song for me.

We know that the moonsnails are at their slow
Secret work. Maybe that old preacher would say,
If he had an MFA in creative writing:
"We are always opened, sometimes by dark
Deliberate drilling, sometimes in gullscream flight.
We are always opened, if we live,

Even by random useless knowledge.
Open, we leave our shells behind at the high-tide

Line, for some stranger to find and proclaim
The perfect ashtray." But I would rather
Hear him pray, in the old way: "Lord teach us
Truly, in Nature, to be Vessels of Love."

Vesselectomy: (Or, Riding the Westbound Train, Contemplating
a Poem for a Journal Deadline, Theme Issue=Vessels)

This train I am riding in is a vessel
The tunnel we are entering is a vessel
The landscape we emerge in is a vessel
The lines I am writing make a vessel
The wine I am drinking passes from vessel
To vessel: so when I empty this glass
Get off the train, destroy these lines,
Go to a dull hotel, no tunnels, no landscape,
No motion, no wine —
Will I perform a vesselectomy?

I asked Vasari and Vasco de Gama
About this: they did not know the answer
Although Vasco was proud of his Vessel.
I asked a man in the bar who looked like
An old seadog. Said he knew vessels, all right.
His favorite navigator was Sir Francis Drake,
He said, who circumcised the world with his bold
Clipper before he was beheaded.
I asked a learned doctor who told me
That there is a vast difference between the vas deferens

And other carrying-off vessels.
I asked Rimbaud, who had emptied too many vessels
In his Drunken Boat. He answered with a pseudo-riddle
"If you write poetry, while drinking wine
And making love and emptying yourself
So the savage gods might enter — are you engaged
In infinite fullness or infinite emptiness?"
Then he started to tell me about his vesselectomy
And I said "Go Vest, Young Man" and started singing
"Here we go a-vesseling. . .Wassail all Vessels of Love."

Toad Suck Ferry: Arkansas 1975

One of the other things
About rivers
        is the crucial business of how you get across
Them.
Give them every chance
Give yourself every chance
To connect.

Not just rivers. Crossing borders,
Oceans, intersections
Where we stop, look, listen;
Crossing years, centuries, millenniums —
                crossing

Sometimes seems like the only authentic
Thing we have left.

We, for example, take
        ferries
Instead of bridges
And we drive miles out of the way to do so.
Once there was a sign: "Toad Suck Ferry, 30."
Laughing and pleased with the name we hurried
Off down the road some thirty odd miles
Out of the way across flatlands while
The sun flattened to a dull red at our backs.
Finally, we pulled up at a sign with the facts:
"Toad Suck Ferry: Closed at Sundown."

Well, it was down, the sun, and there was nothing around
And no one
And no sign of the
        Toad Suck Ferry
Just the grinning gravel landing ramp, empty.

And the wide water,
The wide silent Arkansas.

Sadly, we retreated to the merest bridge
Possessed only of the delight of the name
Cheated of full right to claim it ours, yet
Metathesizing and jumbling joyfully for days,
We playfully fondled the phrase:
Toad Suck Ferry   Toad Suck Ferry

Sequel Twenty Years Later: To a Reader Writing an Essay On an Old Poem of Mine Found in an Old Anthology

the professor wrote to me to say he was working
on an essay about an old poem of mine
since this is a kind of exercise in literary criticism
it will all be in
                    lower-case
with random use of
                    space
and rhyme, rhythm and time

the professor asked why and what and how
the toads sucked i told him i knew that once
but i had forgotten
he asked me where the ferry was and did it still run
i said it never was for me and the point was it did not run
for me but i went out of my way to find it and he should too

the professor asked me if i had structured
the poem according to a spatial
                            design
and did i really mean to say metathesize
or shouldn't i have said
transpositional placement of initial letters
in a unitary sequence of words
thus forcing the reader to hear or say
                            toad-fucked surrey
thus foregrounding the oklahoma subtext of the poem
(was i sure i placed the poem correctly he asked)
and leading the reader to the surrey at the
                            fringe
of the poem, not on top, but
                    subtextual
and the sense of scurrying that informed the poem

i wrote back to say that actually i had been
in a beat-up MG convertible with a frayed top
that he might construe as surrey-fringe but i had not put
                            that in the poem

i also said i detested the word "scurry" that i had
never seen a toad
                    scurry
 and i doubted they did and i was quite certain that the
                              ferry
was in arkansas not oklahoma
i told the professor that my real subject was
                                    crossing
that the poem existed under the Sign of the Cross-
ing that he could take his oklahoma subtext and roger
it with his hammerstein that i hoped his putting his mouth
all over my poem with his scurrilous prose did not get him tenure
that the 70s, perhaps you remember that age of yore,
was really a time of greater delicacy for
                              crossings
                                    doublecrossings
                         toads
                              and ferries.

Notebook Entries for Prosepoem

I

The only way to escape the arbitrary is to impose the arbitrary. (When I wake up thinking this, as if it were the eleventh commandment, I know it is in response to some poet or philosopher I have read recently, but I forget who. Still, before my first cup of coffee, it has the force of fiat, the weight of law.)

II

Spontaneity, the sudden joyful following of random impulses, is as a settled mode of living a form of slavery. For the writer, as for all of us, in an age of joyless pseudo-spontaneity, in which the besetting writerly (and human) sins are vagueness and faux-spontaneity, or inspiration, or liberation of the subconscious, or surrealism, or automatism, or many bastard avatars of these once-valuable notions, the bondage of the spontaneous, the lickspittle solipsistic enslavement by the ostensibly self-generated randomness of things, are the greatest obstacles to the necessary simultaneity of precision and vision, exactitude and amplitude.

III

True and joyful spontaneity, which occurs only within a profoundly and ritually ordered deep structure, has been almost lost, dissipated in this Age of Talkshow Aesthetics.

IV

Since I am already on my third cup of coffee, and sitting on the porch observing the garden instead of in my study writing, and since I am still thinking of the things I woke up thinking, I will probably not write a poem today. Never tell your dream before breakfast, they say, or it will come true. Since I do not eat breakfast, as a rule, the proverb must be "Get rid of your dreams before the third cup of coffee or you will not write a poem." Yet just now, in the deep form and porch-design and particularity and singleness of this day, I hear the unexpected birdsong, see the sudden slanting flight low over the hollyhocks. This reminds me that I must soon gather the hollyhock and nasturtium seeds. And that reminds me it is almost October, time to plant my garlic crop. Every First of October, I plant my garlic crop. Every Bastille Day I harvest, braid and hang my garlic crop. We eat the last of the old year's crop the week before the new comes in; we know which varieties to grow, which ones will endure and how to store them, and in what sequence we should eat them. Because of such knowledge, such action, there is spontaneous joy in every random taste.

Everything that truly happens, happens within such deep design. Without the design, nothing truly happens.

V

OK, Borges, why am I thinking of you as I feel (unthinking) the design of my garlic crop? Why am I thinking of you when I have not read you in maybe twenty years? Did you somehow figure in my dreams — I no longer know, since I am on my fourth cup of coffee.

VI

OK, Borges, everything that has ever happened happens now, is happening now in the absolute subjective present. And yes, Time can be over-determined by Will. And the Future can be made nearly as irrevocable as the Past. And you can play, Borges, with your forked time, your web of divergent, convergent and parallel forms of Time. All this, any thinking schoolchild realizes, some notion of infinite contemporary universes in which all possibilities are realized in all possible combinations. Kidstuff, I say, and necessary to move beyond. Maybe to this, maybe to that — exact knowledge of and feeling for the path you have chosen as it has chosen you. . .Maybe a Ritual Garlic Crop.
Did you eat much garlic, Borges, did you grow your own? And then there is the fatal flaw. Since your Garden of Forking Paths contains all possible experiences, it does not matter to you that on one path you murder someone, because on another path you embrace him as friend and brother. This is the kind of nonsense and pseudo-philosophizing that has gotten all of us in a lot of trouble. You forget, Borges, that all the paths, however multiplicitously forked, are in your Garden; you want to forget that a murder on any path in your Garden is a murder that reverberates to all paths in the ultimate Garden. You want to forget that you are responsible, you are the Gardener. You cannot erase that with an easy quasi-Einsteinian embrace. This dead horrific century has tried all that and look where we are now, where we have been, where we still are.

VII

A mulberry leaf drifts lazily, maybe haphazardly, down and into my empty coffee cup on the porch railing. A robin flies purposefully to the nest in the evergreen above the hammock at the edge of the porch. Perhaps he flies in the Heaviness of Being. I salute him with a cuckoo Kundera-bird call of being. Didn't Valéry say: *Il faut être léger comme l'oiseau, et non comme la plume?* The feathery lightness of things does not really interest me, usually bores me, repels me. The flight of birds and our deep longing for flight is another thing, however. These things may or may not be related, dear Valéry — perhaps your connection is dubious. Is the bird in flight exhilarated by its lightness of being? disdainful of the heaviness of earth? proud in the sleight-slanted weight of its will? Or is the act of flying completely unrelated to any notion of lightness? Is flying about direction and destination, takeoff and landing, finding and feeding? And sometimes just about flight. Probably all of the above. But in the Multiple Choice of flight, it is never about some romantic fantasy of lightness.

VIII

Yes, OK, life can be over-determined by Will. It can also be over-determined by poverty, by wealth, by revolution, by natural disaster, by random biological events (e.g., children), by accident and by confused vocational choice. What is most distressing these days, however, the veritable end-of-millennium mark of identity, is the under-determination of life, the drift into what we call the Future. The disappearance of the Shaping Will. Most people live vaguely, drift randomly into last-minute concatenations, unable to project themselves into a shapely Future. This phenomenon has its everyday manifestations in the inability of most people to commit to a plan for next week, next month, next winter, next year, or even to remember tomorrow the vague plan they made yesterday. Words are no longer deeds. When nothing is translated into action, all becomes vague, ambiguous, equivocal, obscure, and life is shapeless. In this depressing morass of vagueness, when random soggy action does occur, it is sentimentalized as spontaneity, romanticized as freedom. The fact that I know two years in advance exactly when and where I will give a poetry reading in France, or a lecture in Greece, gives shape to the Future, definition not limitation, a structure within which I can exercise my radical freedom, can know truly what the vague Prophets of the Eternal Present, of the Nowness of Things, are pleased to celebrate as Spontaneity.

IX

Seamus Heaney sometimes seems like an old friend or brother, especially when I read him going down to sleep. (I've never met him, but people tell me I look like him. So what — they also say I look like Kenny Rogers and Steve McQueen and Ernest Hemingway. I don't look like any of them, but it's sometimes hard to know what name to sign when strangers approach you in the streets for autographs.) Last night my brother, old dream-shamus talked to me in my sleep saying our countries are different, our cities are different, but still the same. We know many things together, the details, the truck of life, the ruck and moil of time, and the knowing is synchronous. Last night in dreams he waved to me from a great distance on a particular country lane that we both knew very well. We approached each other slowly in our place-immersion,

our Devotion to the Local, as if that country lane were the Deus Loci and all th
countryside were Time. As the dream ended, we were about to shake hands —
his arm was raised to the sky and he shouted something that sounded like
"Yippee!" I woke up this morning hearing his shout, then remembering that
somewhere he refers to "Ghost Riders in the Sky" as "The Riders of the
Range." And I wondered if we really were brothers, after all. And he spells
Yippee-iaaa as "Yippee-i-ay," so I wonder if he can sing at all, if he has a tin
ear? Or is that just because he was born in 1939 and thus missed meeting the
real Ghost Riders at the exactly correct moment (which is like missing Elvis in
1955 or Dylan in 1962, those exact moments when the world shifted and only
people born in 1941 can truly feel and understand.) Yeah, right. That's a fine
theory. Tin ears and momentary lapses of exactitude in observation (or maybe
just static on an old radio outside Belfast or the alterations of oral tradition)
account for more missed grace-notes and earth-shifts than asynchronousness.
Time and simultaneity do matter, but you can always adjust it a few years eithe
way. And forget tin ears. So, with my first cup of coffee, I sing this for you,
Seamus Heaney — "Ghost Riders in the Sky" — our song of brotherhood.

X
In a dream a voice said: "Where the dead men gather to piss in dark alleys."
That was all there was to the dream, separate, complete, oracular. I did not
know what it meant or who said it. It seemed connected somehow with the nex
remembered dream: a girl in Moscow flirted with me then bought me lunch at
the old Metropole Hotel. Then she loaned me her motorcycle. I rode through
the streets of Moscow in the bad old days, conscious of the samizdat manu-
scripts I was going to smuggle to Paris, bouncing like an albatross in my
backpack. Then there was a roadblock, many police, and the girl who bought
me lunch and loaned me her motorcycle was there, pointing at me and scream-
ing "Thief!"
Then she laughed, her eyes still flirting with me, as they took me away to jail.
That was it, all there was to the dream, separate, complete, oracular. (There
was a related dream-vignette in which some publisher said: "Couldn't you write
'urinate' instead of 'piss'? Or maybe 'pee'?" No, I said, those words were not
possible, were ridiculous, for different reasons, and besides that's not what the
dream-voice said. When I woke up I knew this dream did not matter, but the
other two did.) There seemed to be a poem in the first two dreams, and a
connection I had to figure out. Does it mean that dead motorcyclists gather to
piss in dark Moscow alleys? I don't think so. And I never rode a motorcycle in
Moscow. I did have a fine lunch at the Metropole in 1984, with my wife. I was
going to take some manuscripts to Paris, until the CIA-man told me it was too
dangerous and he had a more secure route. I have pissed in many dark alleys,
but never, as far as I know, with dead men. Before my third cup of coffee I

will try to divine the connections: will and spontaneity, words and deeds, birds and Borges, garlic and Valery, Heaney and "Ghost Riders," Moscow and motorcycles, mysterious girls and manuscripts, dead men pissing in dark alleys. On second thought, maybe it's all too obvious. I'll leave that for some reader to explain. Besides, there are still five cups of coffee left in the pot. I'll drink all of it while I plan my garlic crop.

Map-rapt, I Walk Out of the Atlas and Into the World

(for Jerry Jeff Walker, still singing:
Sort of an Answer-Song to "Stoney")

For eight years, from age four
(Or maybe before, from the coiled cartography of the womb)
In a cold, unheated bedroom
I studied the Bible of the Road,
Memorized the Scripture of Rivers
In my favorite book, The Atlas.
The rivers and roads ran through my sleep,
The black lines of railroads, the blue curve of streams,
The red routes of highways,
Rioted in my waking dreams.
The bright shapes of states
And commingling countries shifted in the clouds.
Then, at age thirteen,
   Map-rapt,
   I walked out of the Atlas and into the world.

Ah how shall I now name that quality of terrestrial faith
We no longer have, that sweet telluric singing innocence:
To head for nowhere and everywhere
With no money and little sense,
The only ticket the guitar on my back.
The streetsmart heart grown roadwise
In the thumb and the thrum of the dissonant distance,
For twelve years I merged, singing, with all the maps.
I had vowed to hitch-hike and freight-hop
A million miles before I was 21.
Long before that, after 48 States
And a handful of countries,
I stopped counting the borders, the miles:
   Space-rapt,
   I walked in the world, rambled beyond all maps.

Then, in mad hunger for the calculus of place,
I no longer raged to devour mere space. Singing the ballads
Of strange bars and barns, the lyrical laments
Of the road with nameshifting road-friends,
I woke up one morning in a stranger's barn

At sunrise and knew that I had discovered Time
And Place. Then, for a dozen years,
Insistently rooted, stubborn anachthon in countryside,
I cultivated the wayward domestic joy,
The restless and radical fact of the two great truths:
Home   The Road
I cashed in my oneway ticket to tomorrow,
Purchased a roundtrip ticket to yesterday,
A permanent Eurailpass into history.
All the trains and the ships and the planes
Of Europe and Asia led me to optative homes:
I settled, living, folding into the ancient gnomic names —
Paris, Provence, Peking:
       Time-rapt,
       I sang chthonic chants and burned all the maps.

From birth, the form of the world
Gave a shape to my heart's seeking.
Till death, the dirt of the vast earth
Gives green grace to fortunate footfall.
Violent Victory Gardens of felicity
Map hieratic harvests of complicity.
Yet still, around the road-weary world,
Around the wind-rambling, rail-dancing, ship-delighted world,
Knowing that a man's Word is his Road,
I search for that guitar-shaped country
Where a man's Song is his Deed:
       Place-rapt,
       I compose the incarnational Atlas, the one bright book

Of Particularity. So now and tomorrow,
For all the unmapped moreness of the years,
I acknowledge and follow that need.
At some far Crossroads, where strangers greet me
Like some Prodigal Son, I drink from their springs,
I kneel into an old dream of new maps.
I bow again to the original gods of the Atlas,
I chant the boy's prayer, present the old man's petition:
Let me die on one continent
And be buried on another,
Singing somewhere on the Road near Home:
       Map-rapt,
       I walk out of the Atlas and into the World.

Cartographers of the *Deus Loci*

Directive: This is how you find the Mill House,
How you seek the Spirit of this Place. Leave
New York, under the sulphurous sun of our century,
Leave the detritus and debris
Of an epoch of enterprise and waste,
Find the Great North River of the Indians,
Mystical mother-which-flows-two-ways, Mother
Hudson: She leads through the unhoused landscape,
The unpardonable topology of our works and days,
She tacks along the banks of acid winds
To the mouth of Jew's Creek, where our tale begins:

Marlborough. 1714. Lewis Moses Gomez:
Sailed the vast Sephardic seas with visions
Of ample Americas. Came here to build
A generous place of stone, a trading post,
Where Indians came softly down from the hills
On the ancient Danskammer trail
To trade with Gomez by the great fireplaces,
Under the furs hanging from the broad beams,
Under the virgin scenes of this green Eden.
We see you there, Gomez, attending the voice
Of the numinous land; we are with you
As you incline one ear to the *deus loci*,
The other to the insidious susurrus of history:
            Ah, Gomez,
            When the wild onions
            Began to perfume the fields
            Were you troubled
            By memories of the Courts of Castile?

It is impossible, now, to say how it was for you,
Scion of counselors of Kings. We know only this:
You came to this place, built a house of local
Enduring stone. In the records of the region
You are known as "Gomez the Jew."
The records of the continent read:
"This is the oldest Jewish house in North America."

A voice says:
"This then is the Jewish Plymouth Rock."
Oh the maps all agree,
Charting your song beyond Scylla's reef
Beyond the cloistered voices
And memories of the clustered vines
Of Rioja and all Marrano wines:

By your solid door, the creek, like enfabled time,
Still flows over and under your name: Jew's Creek.
      Rock, stone, time, hieratic creek
      If we listen, the *deus loci* will speak

After you came Wolfert Acker, of Dutch blood
Deeprun in the Hudson Valley.
Revolutionary patriot, ardent after Tories,
He shaped place and time, built well on your foundation,
Added to your stone, good brick stories.
The tale moves well, clear and true: Yes, Gomez,
Acker presided at the birth of the nation
That you had dreamed here in the wilderness.

The 1800s came and the land filled up with farms;
Then great estates and country houses
Began to shout from the banks of the Hudson.
But here, a man of quiet taste came, preferring
Something modest, something solid: Armstrong,
His name, of a family of artists and statesmen.
Novelist, gentleman farmer, sportsman,
His ear attuned to the domestic hosanna
Of the venerable Gomez hearth:
He was a long and loving tenant
Cultivating a pastoral pleasance.
      Against the raging tide of history,
      He dreamed of *otium cum dignitate*.
      And to him, Gomez, what did your stones say?

Still, now, in this century, the special
Dispensations, accidents or blessings
Of history have provided careful stewards
To nourish, to guard,

The vision, the stones,
The lessons of endurance and blessedness
The image of Gomez
Daring to dream and to work in the wilderness:

There has been Dard Hunter, artist, craftsman,
Paper maker known round the world.
He came here, rebuilt the ruined mill in Jew's Creek,
Made a Devonshire Cottage, made the water work.
Deep in a dream of the beauty of handmade books
He labored with dipping-vat,
Rag-duster, rag-boiler, great press,
Punch-cutting, matrix-adjusting, hand-casting:
The dream's maceration
In the sweating facts, in the mill
And the moil of beauty's laceration.
A maker he was, and the sheets are pressed:
The radiant paper, like luminous history,
Is hanging to dry in the loft.

This rich matrix summons the Word,
The Deed, and all these have come here,
And others, makers and doers, adding a line,
A stanza, a variant melody
To the ancient enduring song of the *deus loci*.

So now, here in this rare place we stand,
Pilgrims, attending to the voice of the land,
The labor of human heart and hand.
The twentieth century, weary, leans in against us.
The jaded, besmirched myth of progress
Leers among rumors of landfills, quarries,
Power plants, toxic farms and polluted creeks,
Simpers and fondles the unfished stream where trout
No longer rise through pesticides and stercorry.
We are rocked in the songstopped ear, among the sirens
Of dark tomorrows, caught in the tension
Between pastoral and tragedy,
Caught in the savage Arcadia of the 1980s.
           We ask: will we have the courage
           To see that this place endures?

We ask: will we have the knowledge
To dream the dream of tomorrow?
For without the facts of the past
There is no dream of tomorrow
For without the artifacts of the past
There is no form for tomorrow

Pilgrims, study the work of these cartographers:
Here are the charts, the beams, the hieratic stones.
They may teach us how to build, how to make,
How to endure, how to create.
Here, in the bright particularity of place,
We may hear the oracle of the *deus loci*
Telling us all we may know of blessedness.
We may hear Gomez singing in the wilderness.

(1982)

II
Cartographers of the Deus Loci: Sequel 1999
(for Nan Cullman Boas, Michael H. Cardozo IV, Dard Hunter,
Frances Low, & Joe Cullman)

We dreamed, we met, we planned, we acted:
Family descendants, poets, power-brokers,
Disciples of the Deus Loci.
Many tribes from many places all made one
In the community of history and place.
Many lectures, poetry-readings, fund-raising
Dinners. Time is salvaged, Place is saved.
(I always knew that Poetry preserves Place
But I didn't know that Poetry raises cash.)

The oracle spoke — "Fiat" — and this we have done.
Today, schoolchildren visit the museum,
Refugees from a timeless, placeless present:
At least they have this chance to see,
To feel the intricacy of history,
To celebrate the festivals, know the facts, feel the truth.
Let them take a dream of action, place and freedom,
Take it with them into the next Millennium.
We acted. Let them act. This we have done.

(1999)